D0397691

Extreme Makeover

Teresa Tomeo

Extreme Makeover

Women Transformed by Christ,
Not Conformed to the Culture

IGNATIUS PRESS   SAN FRANCISCO

Cover photograph:
Mammuth/istockphoto.com

Cover design by Riz Boncan Marsella

©2011 by Ignatius Press, San Francisco
All rights reserved
ISBN 978-1-58617-561-0
Library of Congress Control Number 2011926369
Printed in the United States of America ♾

Speak in the Light*

Archbishop Charles J. Chaput
of Denver Colorado

Cardinal Henri de Lubac once wrote that "It is not true
... that man cannot organize the world without God. What
is true, is that without God, [man] can ultimately only organize it against man. Exclusive humanism is inhuman humanism."...

Living within the truth means living according to Jesus
Christ and God's Word in Sacred Scripture. It means pro-
claiming the truth of the Christian Gospel, not only by our
words but by our example. It means living every day and
every moment from the unshakeable conviction that God
lives, and that his love is the motive force of human history
and the engine of every authentic human life. It means
believing that the truths of the Creed are worth suffering
and dying for.

Living within the truth also means telling the truth and
calling things by their right names. And that means exposing the lies by which some men try to force others to live....
The world urgently needs a re-awakening of the Church in

* Archbishop Charles J. Chaput, "Speak into the Light", *Magnificat*, July
9, 2011, pp. 129–31. Reprinted with permission. Excerpts taken from the
full original text from Archbishop Chaput's address in the first session of the
15th symposium for the Canon Law Association of Slovakia, "Living within
the Truth: Religious Liberty and Catholic Mission in the New Order of the
World", August 24, 2010 (Spisske Podhradie, Slovakia), http://
www.archden.org/index.cfm/ID/4396.

our actions and in our public and private witness. . . . We need to *really* believe what we *say* we believe. Then we need to prove it by the witness of our lives. We need to be so convinced of the truths of the Creed that we are on fire to live by these truths, to love by these truths, and to defend these truths, even to the point of our own discomfort and suffering.

We are ambassadors of the living God to a world that is on the verge of forgetting him. Our work is to make God real; to be the face of his love; to propose once more to the men and women of our day, the dialogue of salvation. . . .

The form of the Church, and the form of every Christian life, is the form of the cross. Our lives must become a liturgy, a self-offering that embodies the love of God and the renewal of the world. . . .

Let us preach Jesus Christ with all the energy of our lives. And let us support each other—whatever the cost—so that when we make our accounting to the Lord, we will be numbered among the faithful and courageous, and not the cowardly or the evasive, or those who compromised until there was nothing left of their convictions; or those who were silent when they should have spoken the right word at the right time.

CONTENTS

"What I tell you in the dark, utter in the light; and what you hear whispered, proclaim upon the housetops. And do not fear."

—Matthew 10:27–28

ACKNOWLEDGMENTS

I have many people to acknowledge for this book—first and foremost my wonderful husband, Dominick. Without your support, faith, and love my own "extreme makeover" would never have happened. I love you, and when I think of all you have done and continue to do for me and our marriage I can only recite the words of Saint Paul in Ephesians 1:16: "I do not cease to give thanks for you, remembering you in my prayers".

To my daddy, Michael, who was born on the feast of the Annunciation, March 25, 1926, and passed on from this life on the feast of Our Lady of Sorrows, September 15, 2010: *Lo vi amo e mi manchi.* I love you and I miss you. Thank you for always reminding me that I could do whatever I chose to do as long as I was willing to work and study hard. Thank you also for teaching me that all men and women are created equal and deserve to be treated with dignity. You told me "everyone puts their pants on one leg at a time and no one was any better than anyone else regardless of their status in life". Your sound advice continues to make a difference in my work, especially now as a Catholic journalist. Daddy, pray for me.

To Ma, my mother Rosie. Thank you for showing me that real beauty begins on the inside and in turn leads to beauty on the outside. You are one of the most beautiful women I know, inside and out. Thanks also for keeping me humble and for never letting me forget my roots, and most of all for the sacrifices you and Daddy made to bring me up in the Catholic faith. I love you.

To the amazing team at Ignatius Press for believing in me and in this book project and for providing so much help and support. Thank you Mark Brumley, Father Joseph Fessio, S.J., Anthony Ryan, Diane Eriksen, Eva Muntean, and everyone at Ignatius. I am proud to be an Ignatius author.

To my dear friend and fellow Catholic author Cheryl Dickow, who was with me from the beginning on this project. Your friendship, feedback, and input mean the world to me.

To Amy, Marissa, and Gail; thanks for all your great work with Teresa Tomeo Communications and especially your amazing efforts to promote this book. You're the best.

And last but not least to the women who were bold enough to share their testimonies for our "Let's Hear It for the Girls" chapter: Janet, Astrid, Kathy, Nina, Mary Lockwood, and Mary Dudley. I know your stories will touch so many women. Thanks for joining me in my effort to help others experience their own extreme makeover.

Chapter 1

What's a Girl like Me Doing in a Church like This?

Teresa's Testimony

How in the world did I get here? That was the big fifty-thousand-dollar question running through my mind as I sat in the audience at a Vatican women's congress in February 2008.[1] I was somehow chosen as one of some 280 delegates from around the world to attend this important event dealing with women's issues. The event marked the twentieth anniversary of John Paul II's groundbreaking document *Mulieris Dignitatem* (*On the Dignity and Vocation of Women*). I remember the excited anticipation as I jumped in the cab, headed to Detroit Metropolitan Airport, and boarded my flight for Rome. My head was spinning and my heart was bursting with all the events in my life, including an enormous U-turn, that had led to that invitation. It all seemed—and still seems in so many ways—surreal.

There is an old saying: Life is what happens when you're making plans. There is another saying that is even more applicable to my situation and more aptly describes my journey to the Rome congress and beyond: If you want to make God

[1] International Convention on the Theme "Woman and Man, the *Humanum* in Its Entirety" (Vatican City, February 7–9, 2008).

laugh, make plans. The Lord is probably still laughing—or at least grinning nonstop—as He watches this former women's libber and secular journalist take to the Catholic airwaves each day, as well as to the Catholic speaking circuit several times a month, to tell as many people as she can—especially women—that she was wrong and that the Church was—and is—right! This, mind you, is coming from someone who walked away from her cradle Catholicism and didn't look back for more than fifteen years. This is coming from someone who could barely name the seven Sacraments and who had cracked open a Bible maybe only once or twice in her life. I barely knew the difference between the Old and the New Testaments because the Church and the Bible weren't even on my radar screen.

Well, okay, there was actually a Bible on a table somewhere in my parents' home, but the only time I went looking for it was when I was choosing the readings for my wedding Mass. I couldn't tell you why it was so important for me to get married in the Church since I was barely practicing my faith. But that's what so many of us did and still do: treat the Church's Sacraments as rituals that help us celebrate the big events in our lives but do not signify any serious relationship with Christ. We cradle Catholics often want, and even feel entitled to, the picture-perfect Church wedding with all of the trappings and none of the commitments. In my case, I was unserious about my faith because I was too busy in the seventies and eighties listening to the ravings of radical feminists who were rallying in Washington and just about everywhere else.

These feminists claimed to be changing society so that women could have it all: career, marriage, and children. Though clamoring for women to enter the workforce, they said a woman would still be able to stay home with her children, as long as family life was really her choice. As we soon found out, however, those women who did choose the house over the U.S. Senate, so to speak, were left, no pun intended, at home in the dust. The only "real" choice was the feminist fast track. Anything else was seen as meaningless at best, or at worst a wet rag drowning out the "I am woman, hear me roar!" battle cry.

Looking back, I can see that my falling away from the Church was not a onetime decision caused by a particular event or even by a specific disagreement with Church teaching. I was gradually sucked into the newly emerging culture—little by little—and eventually became your typical, politically correct Catholic who saw nothing wrong with contraception and who identified herself as "pro-choice". You know, the "abortion's not for me, but ..." routine.

Adrift on a Sea of Change

I began to drift away from the Church after I graduated from Catholic grade school in 1973. While the lay teachers and the Sisters of Saint Joseph had provided strong catechesis in terms of the basic tenets of the Catholic faith, once I entered high school my formal religious education came to an end. Of course, there was the mandatory Mass attendance with my family, but beyond my religious obligations (which my parents made sure I fulfilled), there was no further teaching. In the seventies, parents still left the primary catechesis up to the Church. Frankly, there wasn't much available for them in terms of teaching tools. Parochial schools and parish life had so far done a fine job passing on the faith, so our parents assumed they would work for their children as well. None of our parents had any idea that the culture would become hostile to the faith and morals of the Church in the latter part of the twentieth century. No one guessed that this new culture would have more influence upon Catholic children than an ordinary Catholic upbringing.

I realized as a young child that I would someday be pursuing a career in communications. My gift for gab was discovered at an early age, and the good sisters decided that they had to put the energy of this "Chatty Cathy" to good use somehow. So they would often call upon me for reading exercises, and they put me in many a school production. My first taste of the spotlight came during a Christmas pageant, when I had to read a short Christmas poem in front of the entire school body:

> Christmas is a tree with lights all aglow.
> Christmas is a candy cane with fresh and glistening snow . . .

As I performed this little number in the third grade, I fell in love with being in front of an audience. Although I can honestly say I also fell in love with Jesus when I made my First Holy Communion, my love for Jesus wasn't nurtured by my teachers like my love for communications was. Any relationship needs to be nurtured. It has to be truly understood not only from a heart perspective but also from a head perspective. While no one had to do much convincing in my case regarding the Eucharist being the Body of Christ, how was I going to benefit from the source and summit of the faith if my love for Jesus in the Blessed Sacrament wasn't developed? How any of us could think that we could grow in our faith by barely putting any time or effort into it is beyond me, but that's what so many post–Vatican II Catholics did—and continue to do.

The archbishop of Philadelphia, Reverend Charles J. Chaput, has done an excellent job of addressing the fallout from the osmosis approach to catechesis. In one address given to a Canadian catechetical congress in October 2010, the archbishop compared many of today's Catholics to the

Hebrews in the Old Testament: "Because they failed to catechize, they failed to inoculate themselves against the idolatries in their surrounding cultures. And eventually, they began praying to the same alien gods as the pagans among whom they lived."[2] He went on to tell those gathering for the event in Victoria, British Columbia, that we have the same struggles in the twenty-first century, thanks to our failure to teach ourselves, and each other, what it really means to be a Christian in the Catholic Church.

> If our people no longer know their faith, or its obligations of discipleship, or its call to mission—then we leaders, clergy, parents and teachers have no one to blame but ourselves. We need to confess that, and we need to fix it. For too many of us, Christianity is not a filial relationship with the living God, but a habit and an inheritance. We've become tepid in our beliefs and naive about the world. We've lost our evangelical zeal. And we've failed in passing on our faith to the next generation.[3]

So there I was in high school unprepared for the tests to my faith that were looming on the horizon. I was encouraged by my teachers to pursue my communications interests—which I did with a passion. That was the Watergate era, when the power of investigative journalism was being played out before everyone's eyes. I desired to be like Bob Woodward and Carl Bernstein at the *Washington Post*. I wanted to change the world for the better as a broadcast journalist, and I admit that the ego also was looking forward to center stage in terms of being in front of the camera and behind the microphone.

---

[2] "Repentance and Renewal in the Mission of Catechesis" (Tri-diocesan Catechetical Congress, Victoria, British Columbia, October 15–16, 2010), http://www.archden.org/index.cfm/ID/4728.

[3] Ibid.

At the same time, I was also leaving God behind in an attempt to pursue my own interests. I was doing just fine on my own, thank you very much, working on the high school newspaper, winning forensics competitions, and even landing a stint on the high school radio station. My Catholicism was something to do on Sundays with Mom and Dad. This pattern continued into college, and pretty soon, since Mom and Dad were three hours away, Mass became a necessity only when I needed a favor from God. How many times do many of us go into the bargaining mode? "Dear God, let me pass this test, or get an A on my project, and I promise I will be a better person and get more involved in my faith."

I would then be off on my merry way thinking I had fed the "one-armed bandit". I had put in my "church tokens" into the spiritual slot machine and hoped that the payoff would be a big one. Other than that, anything having to do with faith was disappearing from my rearview mirror as I went full speed ahead into the world. The road on which I was traveling—this way of thinking only about me, myself, and I—helped me gain a good deal of professional success, but it would also almost cost me my marriage—and more important, my soul. I heard someone say once that the word *ego* is really an acronym for "easing God out", which is exactly what I was doing.

The sexual revolution and radical feminism, which had exploded on university campuses in the 1960s, had become entrenched in academia by the time I was a college student in the late seventies and early eighties. Unfortunately, the mass media had jumped on the liberation bandwagon and was giving full and unquestioning support to the self-proclaimed social reformers calling for an end to traditional sexual morality. They did their best to drown out the voice of the Church, especially when it came to the issue of contraception.

As I went through my college years in journalism school, earning my degree and gaining loads of job experience at news outlets both on and off campus, I was convinced that due to the demanding and competitive nature of the news business, marriage would have to be put on the back burner and might never be practical for someone in my chosen profession. I didn't seek a serious, long-term relationship that could lead to marriage and sought short-term gratification instead. Along with sexual promiscuity comes contraception. Ave Maria Radio host Father John Ricardo, a priest in the Archdiocese of Detroit, says, "God hates sin for one reason. It's bad for us." The word *sin*, or more precisely the words *mortal sin*, at that time had not yet made it onto my vocabulary list. Somewhere in the back of my mind, I knew what the Church taught about contraception and premarital sex. But my conscience had been desensitized by the trivialization of sex that I saw all around me. My life was about my needs and desires. I thought that doing what I wanted, when I wanted, and with whom I wanted represented freedom— the freedom that the Gloria Steinems and the Helen Gurley Browns of the world were always talking about in *Ms.* and *Cosmopolitan* magazines. Pope Benedict XVI summed up the damage done by this approach to freedom in his address to those of us attending the 2008 Vatican women's congress: "Therefore, when men and women demand to be autonomous and totally self-sufficient, they run the risk of being closed in a self-reliance that considers ignoring every natural, social or religious bond as an expression of freedom, but which, in fact, reduces them to an oppressive solitude." [4]

[4] "Address of His Holiness Benedict XVI to the Participants in the International Convention on the Theme 'Woman and Man, the *Humanum* in Its Entirety'" (Clementine Hall, Vatican City, February 9, 2008), Holy See website, http://www.vatican.va/holy_father/benedict_xvi/speeches/2008/february/documents/hf_ben-xvi_spe_20080209_donna-uomo_en.html.

God Threw Me a Life Preserver

Thankfully, the old saying I mentioned earlier—if you want to make God laugh, make plans—would keep playing itself out in my journey. My determination to remain single for the sake of my career was thrown for a loop just two weeks after my college graduation when God brought my future husband into my life. I would learn later that the Lord was also throwing me a life preserver, as my husband, with the help of the Holy Spirit, would pull me out of despair and back into the Church.

In May 1981 I met a very handsome Italian American named Dominick. Dom, an engineering graduate from Penn State, was hired by a Detroit firm in 1980. It just so happened that several family members, including my father, uncle, and brother-in-law, all worked for the same company. My brother-in-law who worked next to Dom showed him my picture one day. Dom mentioned that he would like to meet me, and the rest, as they say, is history. We were engaged in 1981, six months after I graduated from college, and we were married in 1983.

Dom was brought up in the same environment as I was. He was Italian and Catholic. He served as an altar boy in his parish in Scranton, Pennsylvania. He too fell away from his faith in college, and although we were married in the Catholic Church, neither of us really paid much attention to Church teachings. We believed all we had to do was be nice people and we would be just fine. We were also not practicing Church teaching regarding contraception. The selfishness of holding back—of using God's gift of sexuality for gratification instead of for unification and procreation—would lead to a number of marital problems and an overall assumption that matrimony was pretty much a quid pro quo, contractual type of commitment rather than the total self-giving covenant meant by the Catholic Sacrament of Marriage. We certainly were far from reflecting the love between Jesus as the bridegroom and the Church as the bride.

When you're young and in love and making money, you think that your life is just about perfect. Dom had a good and steady job at his firm and was moving up the corporate ladder. I was making a name for myself in radio news in my hometown of Detroit and within a few short years landed a major television reporting position at an independent station. Dom and I bought our first home. We had all the trappings of success but didn't have God. We had definitely become, as my pastor likes to say, "Christers" or "C and E" Catholics. You know the type: the fallen-away Catholics who stop in only at Christmas and Easter.

About a year into my new television position, I was offered another opportunity. The news director asked if I would consider working the late shift. This would mean reporting live for the 10 P.M. news five nights a week and also substituting as an anchor. In my head I had already said yes. I had yet to discuss the new shift with my husband, but I knew this would mean more opportunity for greater exposure and maybe even more money. Dom and I barely discussed it. We thought we could easily handle working completely different hours. We were convinced we could make up for the daily separation by grabbing lunch together during the week or spending "quality" time together on the weekends. *What were we thinking?* Well, we weren't thinking; there certainly wasn't any praying or discerning going on before this major decision was made. We just thought we could handle it because we loved each other so much.

It didn't take very long for our marriage—and our lives—to unravel. While on the outside we looked like we "had it all", on the inside we were falling apart. Due to the pressures that come with general assignment reporting, I was often covering breaking news stories that required me to stay at the scene of a murder or a barricaded gunman long after the news was off the air. The cameraman and I needed to be there to roll the cameras as the story happened. At times I wouldn't crawl into bed until three or four in the morning—so much for those cozy and romantic lunches during the middle of the week. Our weekends soon consisted of arguing over household responsibilities—chores that weren't getting done because of the demands of work. Dom also was feeling a lot of on-the-job pressure as he moved into management positions and took on more responsibility. Neither of us kept promises made to the other. Our resentment led to many an unkind word and uncharitable act. As a result, our relationship got worse and worse.

Although radical feminists constantly push the idea of women being able to "have it all", my experience was quite different. Sadly, not only my male managers, but also my female ones, looked down on anyone not willing to give up a home life for the career track. We were regularly reminded that there was always someone prettier—and especially cheaper—who could take our place in a heartbeat. If you complained about the long hours, weekend shifts, or lost vacation days, you were branded "high maintenance" and given low-profile assignments. I found it so hypocritical that an industry that is so quick to criticize the corporate world for bad business practices such as discrimination, harassment, and poor working conditions could never take an honest look at itself.

I'll never forget the very sensitive situation that occurred with a pregnant colleague. In her midforties at the time, she began to experience some medical problems. When she explained to our news director (a woman) that she would have to follow doctor's orders and take some additional time off, the boss told her that she wasn't the first woman to be pregnant on the job and that she needed to "get over it" and get back to work. I received the message loudly and clearly: marriage and family life had to take a backseat. As a result, I was the "go-to" girl when it came to putting in the extra hours, even on holidays. I never thought about the price I would pay in the long run for putting my sacred career in front of everyone and everything else in my life. And I never thought about the hypocrisy of the so-called feminists or women's libbers: your choice was fine as long as it was the same choice as theirs.

A Providential Invitation

God can use anyone, or any setting, to extend His invitation for conversion or reversion. In our case, He used a Detroit Pistons basketball game. Dom and I were invited by the news director and her husband, Gene, to attend a game at a time when the Pistons were winning back-to-back NBA championships. I couldn't have cared less about sports. But I did care about being seen. These were front-row seats at the Palace of Auburn Hills and would be another sign to the world that I had "made it". Only the who's who of the celebrity world could gain access to such coveted tickets. Despite my husband's love for sports, the last thing he wanted to do was talk shop at a game. He agreed to go only because he knew saying no to my boss would probably not be in my best professional interest. Accepting the invitation turned out to be in the best interest of both of us because it paved the way for a true relationship with Christ and our eventual return to the Catholic Church.

Gene was a radio producer who also happened to be a born-again Christian. He must have sensed some longing—or some need—in Dom, because while I was shaking hands and kissing babies and making sure that the local paparazzi was aware of my presence, Gene began chatting with Dominick and invited him to his men's Bible study. Now, my husband is an engineer, and I always say that it takes him five years to buy a shirt. Dom jokes that he often suffers from the "paralysis of analysis". He thinks about something for a long time before making a decision, and then he thinks about it again. That night, however, he said yes to the invite—and very quickly. Looking back, we realize it was the Holy Spirit moving, as Dom would have never made such an on-the-spot decision.

This men's Bible study changed Dominick's life. His group was studying several books in the Old Testament, including Exodus, Numbers, and Deuteronomy. God used Dom's background as an altar boy to help him see the Catholic Church, namely, the Mass, in Scripture—especially with the many references to the high priest's vestments, the altar, and the tabernacle. Soon after enrolling in the Bible study, he also began to take classes at Sacred Heart Major Seminary in Detroit. He was rediscovering the Church and was enthusiastic to the point of almost hitting me over the head with the Bible and the *Catechism of the Catholic Church*. I, on the other hand, was put off by his zealous approach and kept going in the opposite direction. We were still dealing with the work pressures and the tensions at home, and the closer Dom moved toward God, the more I moved away from my husband. Dom was a conscience check for me. He also started to express concerns about contraception that I was not ready to hear.

While I still loved my husband deeply, I loved my job status as well and didn't see how now, with this "religion thing" thrown into the mix, we were going to make our marriage work. I saw the Church, including her teachings on contraception and abortion, as restrictive and archaic. I had long since bought into contraception and abortion, although I would never call myself "pro-abortion". No, I was "pro-choice". Interestingly enough, my husband—although he too fell away from many Church teachings—was always pro-life. As an engineer and someone with a true appreciation for science, he thought that it was obvious life begins at conception. A woman is pregnant with a child, not a choice.

Serious moral and religious issues were driving a wedge between Dominick and me. Exacerbating this was the lack of time the two of us spent together. And then another fly flew into the already-messy marriage ointment—I became unemployed. One beautiful fall day, I walked into the television studio to report early for work at the request of the news director. The assignment desk didn't say why I needed to come in; I was just informed that the boss needed to see me as soon as possible. Within thirty minutes of arriving, I was walking out the door with a box of personal belongings in my hands. I was fired as part of some fine-tuning often done in the highly competitive television news business. The night before I was standing side by side with reporters from all over the country, including the major broadcast networks, reporting live on a Detroit police brutality case that was making headlines around the nation. When ratings go down, the blame is usually placed on the shoulders of the on-air personalities. I was no longer the flavor of the day. In a few short weeks, others would be let go as well. As I drove home in tears and in shock, I can remember thinking about all the extra hours, the weekends, and the holidays I gave up—and for what? I had sacrificed so much, and all I received was a small severance and an escort to the door.

Dominick was supportive and told me to take all the time I needed to think about what I wanted to do careerwise.

There was no question in my mind. I was going to get back on the air and do what it takes to be the "It-girl" of television news again. Thanks be to God, I at least had some brains left and decided that I also wanted to work on our marriage. I agreed to some counseling, but I wasn't ready to go back to church.

As a matter of fact, I was angry at God. I asked, "If God really loved me, why would He take away the one thing I am really good at?" As the months went by and my phone calls to co-workers and other news directors in town were ignored, I realized that it might be a good idea to use the time I had on my hands not only for job searching but for some soul searching as well. This was a painful process and one that many people avoid, because if you're sincere about self-examination, results come only after a lot of prayer and hard work. Jesus tells us in John 15:1–2 that He is going to prune us so that we may grow. And believe me, this pruning is not the most pleasant of experiences! "I am the true vine, and my Father is the vinedresser. Every branch of mine that bears no fruit, he takes away, and every branch that does bear fruit he prunes, that it may bear more fruit."

Almost six months had gone by since my firing, and I decided that maybe this God thing, this Church that I was baptized in and raised in, might have something to offer me after all. So one day, out of desperation, I simply looked at the crucifix hanging on our bedroom wall and asked God to take over my life. It was a cry for help and direction. Shortly after saying that prayer, I received a call from a top network affiliate in Detroit. They wanted to talk to me about joining their news team as a general assignment reporter. My immediate thought was, "Hey, this Christian thing is great! You say a prayer and get a job. I think I like this." Little did I know that the real work—or the pruning—was just beginning.

Learning to Walk with God

I did take the job at the top network affiliate but not without some long and serious discussions with my husband—and not without prayer. We made a commitment not to let work come between us again. We started to go back to church as a couple and slowly became involved in our parish. Little by little we recatechized ourselves with the help of some wonderful Christian brothers and sisters, both Catholic and Protestant. It was an exciting time for us. We were getting our marriage back on track and, more important, getting right with God. I was slowly beginning to see the beauty of Church teaching, especially where the life and marriage issues were concerned. It was like peeling away the layers of an onion piece by piece.

For several years the excitement continued. My new boss, although not a Christian, recognized that my Catholicism was important to me and encouraged me to cover faith-based stories in addition to my work as a general assignment reporter. This allowed me to report on the Promise Keepers movement, do numerous interviews with Adam Cardinal Maida (then the archbishop of Detroit), and also cover the 1995 visit of John Paul II to the United States. I believed that the Lord had planted me at Channel 7 for a reason and that I would have a long and successful career at a well-respected station in my hometown. Here comes that cliché again: If you want to make God laugh, make plans!

There is a beautiful Scripture verse that I use when giving my testimony at conferences and retreats. It's from the Old Testament Book of Jeremiah: "You will seek me and find me; when you seek me with all your heart, I will be found by you" (29:13–14). I was learning that seeking God and finding Him was not a onetime deal but a daily walk. Sometimes that journey takes us to places we don't want to go or reveals to us issues or problems that we don't want to face. For me, the seeking and finding meant, among other things, realizing that the media industry that I so adored was changing dramatically—and it wasn't positive change. For starters, the news director who hired me was let go and was replaced by what is commonly referred to in the news business as a "bean counter". He was hired with the goal of bringing up the ratings and bringing down the expenses. This type of so-called management was not unique to my place of employment. It was happening in every market, especially in big cities like Detroit where the overhead operations for a news department can be very costly. As a result, the craft of news reporting, which could—when done well—inspire, educate, inform, and promote good, was doing just the opposite.

In my newsroom, and in countless others across the country, the "if it bleeds, it leads" mentality was taking over. Violence, sex, and sensationalism, not to mention fluff or infotainment, made up most of the newscasts. Media bias and imbalanced coverage of anything having to do with faith, especially the Catholic Church, was becoming more blatant, more commonplace. The line between news and opinion was being crossed repeatedly.

At first I ignored this terrible trend, but eventually I knew that it wasn't going away and was most likely only going to get worse. Never could anyone have predicted that the content would be as vile as it is today—not just in the news reporting but in the overall mass media. I knew that I had to make a choice. Either I could stay in the business and try to be some sort of a light in the darkness, or I could leave and use my insider's experience to help others make a difference. I struggled with this for two years, even deciding to give radio one more shot before leaving the secular media behind. Soon I discovered that the environment in secular radio was just as bad as in television; I finally had to choose either to stay or to go. You probably know what I chose.

In February 2000 I decided to start my own communications company to do what I could to counteract the toxic content flooding the media. I didn't know how I was going to make that happen, but I had faith that God would get me there, one step at a time. And that's exactly what He did. My speaking ministry began with an invitation from a friend in public relations. She was relating to me her frustration with the news business. She struggled continuously to promote companies that had good stories to tell about economic development or about volunteer organizations making a difference. It was getting more and more challenging to promote good news of any sort. She was relieved to hear about my efforts in media awareness and thought my perspective would be an interesting one to share with the local chapter of the Public Relations Society of America. The strong reception to that first presentation led to subsequent speaking engagements. Within a few short months, I also received an offer to host my own talk show on the local Christian station. *Christian Talk with Teresa Tomeo* was on the air for two years, and then Al Kresta, a well-known Catholic apologist and host of *Kresta in the Afternoon* and CEO of Ave Maria Communications, brought me over to Ave Maria Radio. Thanks be to God, *Catholic Connection with Teresa Tomeo* has been on the air ever since, and my program, as well as Al's, is now syndicated on more than 170 stations through the EWTN Global Catholic Radio Network.

There is another verse I quote when giving my reversion story. It's from Saint Paul's Letter to the Romans: "We know that in everything God works for good with those who love him, who are called according to his purpose" (8:28).

Note how Saint Paul says "everything". That means not only the things we are proud of but *everything*: the good, the bad, and yes, the ugly. All the experience I gained from more than twenty years working in the news media, from my marriage problems, from my issues with Church teaching that took me years to work through—*everything* is working together for God's glory and for the purpose of promoting the Gospel. For years before my reversion I had been in dire need of an extreme, and I mean a really extreme, makeover. I did not see myself through the eyes of Christ. I was not looking at life through the lenses of Scripture and the teachings of the Catholic Church. As a result, my life spun out of control. There is much more to tell concerning the fallout from my sinful behavior. That will come later, when we take an in-depth look at the issues of radical feminism, abortion, contraception, and poor body image. Suffice it to say that I have learned a few things from my mistakes. I am still learning. God is not through with me yet. But one thing I know for sure: God and His Church have it right. As the late great Archbishop Fulton Sheen once said, "The truth is still the truth even if no one believes it. And a lie is still a lie even if everyone believes it."

The Truth Won Out

The Church contains the fullness of the truth. In this current "dictatorship of relativism", as Holy Father Benedict XVI has said,[5] the ego of the world seems to have taken over. It has eased—or, more appropriately, forced—God out of the picture. It's sad to say that many have accepted

---

[5] Joseph Cardinal Ratzinger [Pope Benedict XVI], homily, Mass "Pro eligendo romano pontifice" (Vatican Basilica, April 18, 2005), Holy See website, http://www.vatican.va/gpII/documents/homily-pro-eligendo-pontifice_20050418_en.html.

the lies of the world as truth. Contraception, abortion, sexual promiscuity, and same-sex relationships are—if you to listen to the mass media—as American as apple pie. In our efforts to be tolerant, we have accepted everything, and we are losing ourselves in the process. We are also losing ourselves by placing status and material wealth above everything else.

I speak from both personal experience and professional experience. As a journalist, media expert, and author, I have been writing, researching, and speaking on cultural issues for more than ten years. Truth can be denied but not suppressed forever. God has designed us a certain way, and when we go against the natural order or law, as I found out, we suffer negative consequences. These are not difficult to see if we open our eyes to reality. The proof is in the pudding, so to speak. There have been more than fifty million abortions in the United States since the 1973 *Roe v. Wade* decision. Sexually transmitted diseases are at epidemic proportions, with nineteen million new STD infections each year in the country. The divorce rate in the United States is double that of other developed nations; nearly 40 percent of all children and 70 percent of African American children are born out of wedlock. With the onslaught of pornography and of sexual content in the media, women are more objectified than ever before. Ironically, the research showing these disturbing trends is done mostly by secular think tanks, professional organizations, and universities, thus lending more credence to the truth of Church teaching, the truth of the natural law.

When all is said and done, it is—and has always been—the Church, starting with Jesus Himself, who offers women true freedom. It was the Church, over the centuries, which was actually promoting true equality for women. More recently, John Paul II, in both his 1988 document *Mulieris*

Dignitatem and his 1995 Letter to Women, called for such things as equal pay for equal work and better support for working mothers. However, the messages in magazines, on television, and in films and newscasts are doing their best to deny—and diminish—the truth and beauty of Church teaching, especially as it relates to women. Women have, in many ways, become their own worst enemies by believing they must act like men behaving badly in order to achieve fulfillment and happiness. Distinguished law professor and pro-life speaker Helen Alvaré stressed this point during her presentation at the 2008 Vatican congress:

> On the one hand, one can see how strong was the temptation to break women out of the limited roles assigned to them in earlier times. But this feminism's response was and remains fundamentally flawed. This type of feminism drew upon the worst features of male behavior for its prescriptions. Thus was the feminist woman urged to be a sexually adventurous, marriage- and children-spurning, money- and career-driven creature.[6]

Beginning in the sixties, women were told through the likes of Helen Gurley Brown that we should use our sexuality to advance our careers and nab the man of our dreams, if that's what we wanted. Listening to such advice, women became what feminists supposedly deplored—focused on being alluring to men. While *Cosmopolitan*, the magazine Brown edited, denounced our being treated as mere sex objects, its nearly pornographic covers and articles screamed a different message. Countless magazines for women and teen girls also began emphasizing sexuality, as did movies, advertisements, and television shows aimed at females. And

---

[6] "The Reduction of Femininity to an Object of Consumerism" (International Convention on the Theme "Woman and Man, the *Humanum* in Its Entirety", Vatican City, February 8, 2008).

what has been the result of all this emphasis on female flesh? Women are more objectified than ever before. As Alvaré explained in Rome, the objectification of women is not all the fault of men.

> This is not confined to the pornography industry or even to commercial advertising or films or television. Rather, ordinary women across the continent buy clothing designed to emphasize or expose those parts of their bodies associated with sex. Many women often also debase themselves with their speech, or by exposing themselves to media which gradually desensitizes them to the proposal that women are beautiful, sexualized objects for consumption.[7]

Where are the feminists when it comes to addressing the topic of objectification of women, especially when, as Alvaré points out, women are often guilty of making a bad problem worse? Isn't this what the bra burners were fighting against? How many of us grew up in the sixties and seventies being told—or telling others—that we, as women, were more than just body parts?

According to a 2009 survey from the American Society of Plastic Surgeons, many women believe that in tough economic times a youthful appearance, not hard work or a better résumé, will help secure a job position.[8] It seems that plenty of women have taken the "Cosmo girl" bait. They have bought the message that achieving happiness requires lots of sex appeal, while putting husbands and children on the back burner. Somehow, as you know now, despite buying into this message, I found my way back to God and my

[7] Ibid.

[8] American Society of Plastic Surgeons, "Women in the Workforce Link Cosmetic Surgery to Success", news release, February 10, 2009, http://www.plasticsurgery.org/Media/Press_Releases/Women_in_the_Workforce_Link_Cosmetic_Surgery_to_Success.html.

Catholic heritage. It wasn't pretty, and it wasn't easy. But with God all things are possible. Yes, I was battered and bruised. But I survived. Even more than that, by the grace of almighty God, I blossomed into the woman I was truly meant to be.

The Reason for This Book

That's why I wrote this book—to share with others the transforming power of God's grace. It's not just about my journey but the journey of so many other women like me who were sucked in by the "choices" mantra and found that something essential to their true happiness was missing from their lives. In my first book, *Noise: How Our Media-Saturated Culture Dominates Lives and Dismantles Families,*[9] I took an in-depth look at the media and their influence on families and society. In my research, I began to notice that much of the media is targeted toward women and is being used to get women to accept certain lifestyles and behaviors that are actually harmful to them. Unfortunately, for the most part, the media has been quite successful and has produced a culture that values so-called personal freedom above everything else. As I will document in the chapters ahead, this "freedom" actually leads to all sorts of bondage, greatly impacting the physical, emotional, and spiritual well-being of women.

Unfortunately, many women still don't know about the harm they do to themselves when they embrace the media's definition of freedom. They do not know about the damaging effects of abortion, contraception, sexual promiscuity, and living with a man outside of marriage; nor do they

[9] *Noise: How Our Media-Saturated Culture Dominates Lives and Dismantles Families* (West Chester, Pa.: Ascension Press, 2007).

realize the fallout from believing they have to suppress their natural gifts and abilities and become oversexualized females and at the same time more like men in order to be happy and successful.

I regularly receive e-mails asking for a website, an article, or a statistic regarding a myriad of societal issues, especially those affecting women and girls. My prayer and hope is that *Extreme Makeover* will be a top reference book for women who want to understand what our culture has become and the Church's response. To this end, I've included end-of-chapter reflection questions and a resource guide, as well as a media makeover and spiritual beauty regimen (see chapter 7).

So that's what a girl like me is doing in a Church like this—calling on the One who calms the storms, including the current cultural storm that still rages around us, and on the One who can and does change the world one person, one woman, at a time. He wants you to see yourself as He sees you: as a daughter of the King. It's time for all of us, especially women, to discover or rediscover Christ and the teachings of His Church—and how those timeless messages can transform us, and the world, from the inside out. It's time for an extreme and a heavenly makeover.

> For Zion's sake I will not keep silent,
> and for Jerusalem's sake I will not rest,
> until her vindication goes forth as brightness,
> and her salvation as a burning torch.
>
> —Isaiah 62:1

Chapter 2

Media Mania and the Feminist Mistake

The Mass Media, Radical Feminism, and the Betrayal of Women

Whoever controls the media controls the mind.

—Jim Morrison

Pop music sensation Rihanna, who was at the center of a high-profile domestic violence case in 2009, was featured in a popular music video by rap star Eminem ("I Love the Way You Lie") that glorified the physical and emotional pain of abuse. A scantily dressed Rihanna sang:

> Just gonna stand there and watch me burn
> That's all right cause I like the way it hurts.
> Just gonna stand there and hear me cry
> That's all right because I love the way you lie.
> I love the way you lie.

The November 2010 issue of *GQ*, a magazine targeted toward an adult male audience, printed a hypersexual photo spread of the actresses in the popular television show *Glee*. The women, who portray high school students, were dressed in revealing lingerie and placed in suggestive poses in front of school lockers. The fact that these images suggesting sex with high school girls were directed at adult men was described by one media awareness group as bordering on pedophilia.[1]

In May 2010 the news media portrayed the fiftieth anniversary of the birth control pill as a cause for jubilation and celebration. A front-page story in *USA Today* touted the pill as groundbreaking, a symbol of women's rights, even the catalyst for the women's liberation movement.[2] Research on physical complications and other side effects of the pill, as well as the World Health Organization's classification of the pill as a group 1 carcinogen back in 2005, were downplayed, discredited, or completely ignored by *USA Today* and other major media outlets.

In 2008 Alveda King, the niece of the late civil rights activist Martin Luther King Jr., was silenced during an open-microphone session at a convention of the National Association for the Advancement of Colored People (NAACP) in Detroit, Michigan. King, pastoral associate for Priests for Life, was attempting to raise awareness of the high number of abortions in the African American community, which has lost more than thirteen million lives to abortion since *Roe v. Wade* in 1973. Now, you would think that the secular media would be interested in at least a general interview with the niece of the civil rights giant. And isn't it huge news that she was actually silenced at a convention that is supposed to embody, represent, and promote what her uncle was all about? That sounds like a pretty big deal to me. But it was apparently not a newsflash to the reporters covering

[1] Parents Television Council, "PTC: Sexualized *GQ* Photo Shoot of *Glee* Cast Crosses the Line", news release, October 20, 2010, http://www.parentstv.org/ptc/news/release/2010/1020.asp.

[2] Rita Ruben, "The Pill: 50 Years of Birth Control Changed Women's Lives", *USA Today*, May 7, 2010. (Also available online at http://www.usatoday.com/news/health/2010-05-07-1Apill07_CV_N.htm.)

the conference, as they also, in their own way, muzzled the voice of Alveda King: they ignored her and the other pro-life activists who were there.

A November 2009 report from the Parents Television Council, *Women in Peril: A Look at TV's Disturbing New Storyline Trend*, shows a dramatic increase in the graphic depiction of violence against women. Incidence of violence against women on television jumped 120 percent from 2004 to 2009. In comparison, violence on television overall—irrespective of gender—increased only 2 percent over the same time period.[3]

So have women really made all that much progress? Here we are in the twenty-first century, and despite the increased numbers of women receiving university degrees and entering professions that once excluded them, the sexual exploitation of women and girls seems also to have increased. Why have the media and groups that claim to be on the side of women ignored this alarming trend? Why aren't the National Organization for Women (NOW) and other feminist groups hitting the streets, as their forebears of the sixties did, in massive protest of the way Hollywood and the porn industry portray women? Why aren't the representatives from NARAL Pro-Choice America[4] and Planned Parenthood being honest about the problems with contraception? Why are women's organizations and the media ignoring some of its harmful effects? Why do they turn a blind eye to the cases of statutory rape and state health law violations that continue to surface at abortion centers, especially since they

[3] *Women in Peril: A Look at TV's Disturbing New Storyline Trend* (October 2009), http://www.parentstv.org/PTC/publications/reports/womeninperil/study.pdf.

[4] The acronym NARAL originally stood for the National Association for the Repeal of Abortion Laws; the group changed its name to the National Abortion Rights Action League and then to NARAL Pro-Choice America.

are in favor of abortion being "safe, legal, and rare"? Why aren't these same groups, if they're really all about choice—especially informed choice—concerned about the medical and psychological complications from abortion? Why aren't those who claim to care so much about women's rights open to listening to the stories of women who regret their abortions? Shouldn't organizations such as the NAACP be concerned about how many of their children are being eliminated through abortion and how their race is being targeted by the abortion industry?

No News Is Not Necessarily Good News

These questions continue to go unanswered because, quite frankly, the media sees no need to answer them. Having an abortion, using contraception, and having sex outside of marriage have long been deemed "normal" by the media. With regard to pornography and other ways that women are objectified in the media, for the most part, the powers that be turn a deaf ear or chalk it up to art, freedom of sexual expression, or freedom of speech (a few secular books and articles treat the matter, but they are the exception). Gail Dines, author, sociology professor, and antiporn activist, is one of only a handful of those in academia willing to take a stand against pornography. In an interview with the *Guardian* newspaper in her native Great Britain, Dines, who authored *Pornland: How Porn Has Hijacked Our Sexuality*,[5] gives her take on why she is, for the most part, a voice in the wilderness: "Many on the liberal left adopt a view that says pornographers are not businessmen but are simply there to unleash our sexuality from state-imposed

[5] Gail Dines, *Pornland: How Porn Has Hijacked Our Sexuality* (Boston: Beacon Press, 2011).

constraints".[6] Such a view was expressed in the film *The People vs. Larry Flynt*, in which billionaire pornographer Flynt, founder of *Hustler* magazine, was portrayed simply as fighting for freedom of speech. Dines disagrees with this assessment. "Trust me. I have interviewed hundreds of pornographers and the only thing that gets them excited is profit." There is also fear among her colleagues, Dines explained to the *Guardian*, of being "considered in alliance with the religious right" if they reject pornography. Many scholars hold "the view that pornography represents and champions sexual liberation".

It would seem that these scholars are not alone in their opinion. Producers of news seem to also think that porn is liberating. Research shows how those running the television networks, the newsrooms, and the newspapers have embraced the sexual revolution agenda represented by the NOWs, NARALs, and Planned Parenthoods of this world. In a July 2009 address given in Colorado Springs, Archbishop Charles Chaput reminds us why it's so vital for Catholics, other Christians, and the public in general to realize that those working in the news media do not share their morals or religious beliefs. "The idea that this deep difference in religious practice doesn't flavor our press coverage would be too strange to take seriously. In a sense, we are what we believe. Our convictions shape the way we deal with the world. And that includes media professionals." [7]

The archbishop cited a 2005 study by the Annenberg Public Policy Center showing that 40 percent of Americans

---

[6] Julie Bindel, "The Truth about the Porn Industry", *Guardian*, July 2, 2010, http://www.guardian.co.uk/lifeandstyle/2010/jul/02/gail-dines-pornography.

[7] "Catholics and the 'Fourth Estate'" (address to Legatus chapter, July 8, 2009), http://www.archden.org/index.cfm/ID/2265.

attend weekly church services.[8] When we look at the practices of journalists, that number in the Annenberg report drops to 17 percent. In addition, Archbishop Chaput's concerns are supported by research dating back nearly thirty years. There's the famous Lichter-Rothman survey conducted in 1980, in which news personnel from major media operations, primarily large daily newspapers and major broadcast networks, were questioned about their political persuasions and positions on hot-button issues, including abortion.[9] The vast majority—nearly 90 percent—of those questioned said they were in support of legalized abortion. They also consistently described themselves as left of center. The same study found that half of the respondents had no religious affiliation.

Fast-forward to the twenty-first century and to the work of the Media Research Center, the Pew Research Center for the People and the Press, and others who have been closely monitoring media biases. In 2007 the Media Research Center issued an analysis of the media in terms of journalists' beliefs. The researchers concluded that studies dating back as much as twenty-five years consistently find that journalists are much more liberal than the average American.[10] In 2004 a Pew Research Center report found that five times as many journalists in the United States

[8] "Public and Press Differ About Partisan Bias, Accuracy and Press Freedom, New Annenberg Public Policy Center Study Shows", May 24, 2005, www.annenbergpublicpolicycenter.org/Downloads/IoD_Survey_Findings_Summer2005/Partisan_Bias20050524.pdf.

[9] S. Robert Lichter, Stanley Rothman, and Linda S. Lichter, *The Media Elite* (Bethesda, Md.: Adler and Adler, 1986).

[10] "Financial Woes Now Overshadow All Other Concerns for Journalists, The Web: Alarming, Appealing, and a Challenge to Journalistic Values", Pew Research Center, March 17, 2008, http://people-press.org/2008/03/17/financial-woes-now-overshadow-all-other-concerns-for-journalists/.

describe themselves as liberal as opposed to conservative.[11] Keep in mind that these are the folks putting together the newscasts we watch and the news articles we read. Do you really think we are getting an accurate summary, particularly when it comes to matters of faith and morals?

Matthew Kelly, a devout Catholic and a well-known motivational speaker and author, says, "The way people see the world is the way they live their lives."

Never Let the Facts Get in the Way of a Good Story

While there is ample evidence regarding media bias among journalists, there is even more research to show how the mass media in general attacks Church teaching on a regular basis. Even if the situation comedies or prime-time programs aren't mocking the institutional Church in some way with a character or a story line—which has happened plenty—the media bombards us with messages that mock Christian beliefs, namely, in the area of sexuality and marriage.

When I conduct my media awareness seminars around the country, attendees are shocked at the actual statistics as well as the overwhelming amount of evidence connecting problems in society to media influence. While we certainly can't place the blame for all of our social and moral ills on Hollywood or the *New York Times*, it would be ludicrous to ignore the facts and figures.

According to a 2010 report from the Kaiser Family Foundation, young people are using the media on average some

[11] "Bottom-Line Pressures Now Hurting Coverage, Say Journalists", Pew Research Center for the People & the Press, May 23, 2004, www. people-press.org/2004/05/23/bottom-line-pressures-now-hurting-coverage-say-journalists/.

fifty-three hours a week.[12] Adults aren't doing much better in the media category, consuming at least forty hours of media on a weekly basis. What exactly are young people and adults consuming? Brace yourself. The following statistics are from a 2010 report released by the American Academy of Pediatrics:

- 75 percent of prime-time programs contains sexual content.
- References to sex can occur as often as eight to ten times an hour.
- R-Rated Teen movies since the 1980's have contained at least one nude scene and often several instances of sexual intercourse.
- Between 1997 and 2001 alone, the amount of sexual content on TV nearly doubled.[13]

A 2008 report from the Parents Television Council, *Happily Never After,* found that prime-time television spends more airtime promoting promiscuity and adultery than marital intimacy and fidelity: verbal references to nonmarital sex outnumbered references to sex in the context of marriage by a ratio of nearly three to one.[14] The Parents Television Council also found that on the major broadcast networks, scenes depicting, or implying, sex between unmarried partners outnumbered scenes depicting sex between spouses by a ratio of nearly four to one.

[12] *Generation M²: Media in the Lives of 8- to 18-Year-Olds* (January 2010), http://www.kff.org/entmedia/8010.cfm.

[13] American Academy of Pediatrics, "Sexuality, Contraception, and the Media", October 1, 2010, http://aappolicy.aapublications.org/cgi/content/126/3/576.full.

[14] *Happily Never After: How Hollywood Favors Adultery and Promiscuity over Marital Intimacy* on Prime Time Broadcast Television (August 5, 2008), http://www.parentstv.org/ptc/publications/reports/sexontv/MarriageStudy.pdf.

To say that the statistics on Internet pornography are shocking would be a major understatement. The numbers keep changing—and unfortunately, they are not moving in a downward direction:

- Sex is the number one topic searched on the Internet.[15]
- By the end of 2004 there were 420 million pages of pornography.[16]
- 2.5 billion e-mails per day are pornographic.[17]
- 25 percent of all search engine requests are pornographic.[18]

How about the statistics on media violence?

- A 2009 policy statement from the American Academy of Pediatrics insisted that "exposure to violence in media, including television, movies, music, and video games, represents a significant risk to the health of children and ... can contribute to aggressive behavior." [19]
- A 2010 University of Iowa review of 130 research reports strongly suggests that playing violent video games increases aggressive thoughts and behavior and decreases empathy.[20]

[15] Rebecca Hagelin, "Overdosing on Porn", March 2004, http://www.worldandi.com/specialreport/2004/march/5a23779.htm.

[16] Jan LaRue, "Obscenity and the First Amendment", Summit on Pornography, May 19, 2005.

[17] www.familysafemedia.com/pornography_statistics.html.

[18] David C. Bissette, Psy.D., "Internet Pornography Statistics:2003", http://www.healthymind.com/5-porn-stats.html.

[19] "Policy Statement—Media Violence", *Pediatrics* 124 (November 2009): 1495, http://pediatrics.aappublications.org/cgi/reprint/peds.2009-2146v1.

[20] Craig Anderson, Professor of Psychology Iowa State University, "Violent Video Game Play Makes More Aggressive Kids, Study Shows", *Psychological Bulletin, American Psychological Association Journal* 136, no. 2 (March 2010).

- By age eighteen, your son, daughter, niece, nephew, grandson, or granddaughter will have witnessed sixteen thousand simulated murders.[21]
- By the time the average youth reaches eighteen, he or she will have witnessed two hundred thousand acts of violence on television.[22]
- Over one thousand studies since 1972 show at least a casual connection between media violence and aggressive behavior in some children.[23]

When we step back and take a look at the daily diet of sex and violence that has been fed to the public through innumerable media operations, we shouldn't be surprised by what has happened in our culture, and more specifically what has happened to women. But therein lies the problem. We *don't* step back.

We don't take a second glance or even a closer look. Instead, we go about our busy lives attached to our electronics. We're busy e-mailing, texting, chatting with our Facebook friends, or watching way too much television. On top of all this, Catholics like me—growing up after Vatican II—were poorly catechized or not catechized at all. A weak and uneducated faith is no match for today's mammothmedia, which we let mold our way of thinking and eventually our way of living.

There are some seventy million Americans who identify themselves as Catholics in the United States, but only 22

---

[21] Senate Committee on the Judiciary, "Children, Violence, and the Media: A Report for Parents and Policy Makers", September 14, 1999.

[22] Ibid.

[23] Congressional Public Health Summit, "Joint Statement on the Impact of Entertainment Violence on Children", July 2000, www.aap.org/advocacy/releases/jstmtevc.htm.

percent attend weekly Mass.[24] I don't think it is too much
of a leap to suggest that even those attending Mass are not
spending time visiting good Catholic websites or listening
to Catholic radio to learn more about the teachings of the
Church. As a matter of fact, on a 2010 religious knowledge
survey from the Pew Forum on Religion and Public Life,
atheists, agnostics, Jews, and Mormons scored higher than
Catholics and mainline Protestants.[25] Even more alarming
was the sad statistic showing that more than four out of ten
Catholics—43 percent of those surveyed—did not know that
the Eucharist is not merely a symbol of the Body of Christ
but actually becomes the Body, Blood, soul, and divinity of
the Lord during the consecration at Mass.

A Perfect Cultural Storm

This decline in morals and widespread falling away from
the Church is the result of what I refer to as the perfect
cultural storm of the 1960s, when mass media exploded at
the same time as the start of the women's liberation movement and the sexual revolution. In addition, Catholics saw
open dissent within the Church over *Humanae Vitae*, the
papal encyclical that restated the Church's prohibition of
contraception, as well as confusion about and misinterpretation of the Second Vatican Council. In 1964 the Council
issued its *Dogmatic Constitution on the Church* (*Lumen Gentium*), which provided an understanding of the Church's
nature. In the fifth chapter, members of the Church are
given a specific call: "Therefore in the Church, everyone

---

[24] Center for Applied Research in the Apostolate, *CARA Catholic Poll*
(*CCP*), Fall 2010, http://cara.georgetown.edu/CARAServices/CCP.pdf.

[25] The Pew Forum on Religion & Public Life, "U.S. Religious Knowledge Survey", September 28, 2010, http://pewforum.org/Other-Beliefs-and-
Practices/U-S-Religious-Knowledge-Survey.aspx.

whether belonging to the hierarchy, or being cared for by it, is called to holiness, according to the saying of the Apostle: 'For this is the will of God, your sanctification' (1 Thess 4:3; cf. Eph 1:4)." [26] All of us, men and women alike, were called to change the culture, but as Archbishop Chaput stated in 2009 while in British Columbia, Catholics have changed, and not necessarily for the better: "Instead of changing the culture around us, we Christians have allowed ourselves to be *changed by* the culture. We've compromised too cheaply. We've hungered after assimilating and fitting in. And in the process, we've been bleached out and absorbed by the culture we were sent to make holy." [27]

We are slowly but surely being desensitized by the images and the messages. It's the old analogy of the frog in the pot of boiling water. If you try to kill the frog by throwing him in that pot of boiling water on the stove, he realizes he is in trouble and he jumps out. But watch what happens when you place the same frog in a pot of warm water and slowly turn up the heat. At first he is comfortable, but before he knows it, he's cooked. When I look at the cultural landscape, I can't help but notice an awful lot of female frogs. We are telling our daughters, our sisters, and our friends, "Come on in, ladies; the water is just fine." In the meantime, we are all getting our gooses—or our frog legs—cooked; before we know it, we have all conformed ourselves to this toxic culture of ours. And it is no wonder, considering the size and the powerful outreach of the mass media.

---

[26] *Lumen Gentium* (November 21, 1964), 39, Holy See website, http://www.vatican.va/archive/hist_councils/ii_vatican_council/documents/vat-ii_const_19641121_lumen-gentium_en.html.

[27] "Repentance and Renewal in the Mission of Catechesis" (Tri-diocesan Catechetical Congress, Victoria, British Columbia, October 15, 2010), http://www.archden.org/index.cfm/ID/4728. Emphasis in original.

Toward the middle of the twentieth century, the media began to develop into a massive industry, covering the planet with countless outlets made up of television and radio stations, newspapers, magazines, cable operations, the Internet, cell phones, and other types of communication technology and personal devices. The Catholic Church has always recognized the importance of the media not just for catechetical purposes but also for cultural development, so in 1963—around the same time that the other storm conditions started to form on the horizon—the Second Vatican Council gave us *Inter Mirifica* (*Decree on the Media of Social Communications*). This brilliant summary on the use of the media in the modern world outlined the Church's acknowledgment of media influence and her interest in being a part of something that had the ability to reach the entire human race.

> It is, therefore, an inherent right of the Church to have at its disposal and to employ any of these media insofar as they are necessary or useful for the instruction of Christians and all its efforts for the welfare of souls. It is the duty of Pastors to instruct and guide the faithful so that they, with the help of these same media, may further the salvation and perfection of themselves and of the entire human family. In addition, the laity especially must strive to instill a human and Christian spirit into these media, so that they may fully measure up to the great expectations of mankind and to God's design.[28]

It is mind-boggling to think of just how extensive the media landscape has become. There are some forty-four thousand AM and FM stations around the world, along with twenty-one thousand television stations, not including cable and satellite distributors. A report from the United Nations

[28] *Inter Mirifica* (December 4, 1963), 3, Holy See website, http://www. vatican.va/archive/hist_councils/ii_vatican_council/documents/vat-ii_decree_19631204_inter-mirifica_en.html.

International Telecommunications Union explains that at the end of 2010, a whopping 71 percent of people living in industrialized countries have access to the Internet, with 65 percent of those users connecting at home.[29] Media growth and usage is not a bad thing when, as the Church points out, it's used properly and for the benefit of mankind; but quite the opposite has happened. Although Christian and conservative talk radio outlets are growing, they are still outnumbered by the secular stations. The EWTN Global Catholic Radio Network is growing quickly and continues to add new stations to its affiliate list each year, but as of 2011, there are only about 170 EWTN stations and 30 other independent Catholic radio stations on the air in the United States.

It's not that the Church hasn't been teaching during these changing times; it's that the teachers—up until recently—haven't been able to take as much advantage of the tools that were becoming available. When the media started to expand in the 1960s and 70s, those running the outlets for the most part were running fast and furious away from the Church. While most of the radio and television programs were still quite tame compared to today's standards, the effort to turn society away from the traditional way of thinking about marriage, family, romantic relationships, and the roles of men and women had begun.

Soon after the birth control pill burst onto the scene in 1960, Hollywood began to produce many a film that represented the changes of attitude toward sexual morality. So long, Maria von Trapp; hello, Mrs. Robinson. *The Graduate*; *Goodbye, Columbus*; *Peyton Place*; *Bob and Carol and Ted and Alice*; and *Love Story* were just a few of the box office hits that began to normalize promiscuity.

---

[29] United Nations International Telecommunication Union, *The World in 2010*, http://www.itu.int/ITU-D/ict/material/FactsFigures2010.pdf.

I have mentioned Helen Gurley Brown and her *Cosmopolitan* magazine. In 1962 she wrote *Sex and the Single Girl*. Considered shocking at the time, the book presented extramarital sex with men as a way to achieve personal fulfillment and professional success. But another take on women's lib was brewing at the same time. A year after Brown's book, Betty Friedan penned *The Feminine Mystique*. Calling *Sex and the Single Girl* "obscene", Friedan did not advocate luring men into bed for fun and profit; rather, she focused on what she called "the problem that has no name", that is, the limited lives of suburban homemakers. Friedan's book launched her into the limelight, and she cofounded the National Organization for Women (NOW), which lobbied for the equal treatment of men and women in the workplace, as well as the legalization of abortion

Meanwhile, Gloria Steinem arrived on the scene, writing a report on the birth control pill for the men's magazine *Esquire*. Founding *Ms.* magazine in 1971 and becoming a lead supporter of the Equal Rights Amendment, Steinem ended up one of the main mouthpieces of the radical feminist movement. She made famous the quip, "A woman needs a man like a fish needs a bicycle." She was, and still is, a staunch abortion rights activist.

These and other influential feminists changed the minds of many Americans with regard to sex, marriage, children, and men's and women's roles. As a result, conventions and laws began to change. Laws against discrimination and affirmative action quotas, intended to protect racial minorities, were extended to women. No-fault divorce, abortion on demand, women's ordination in some Protestant churches, and now the push to redefine marriage to include same-sex relationships—all trace their origins to the sexual revolution and the feminist movement.

Mixed Messages

Today, these two movements continue to send very confusing signals to women, as Helen Alvaré pointed out at the 2008 Vatican congress on women. On the one hand, we are told that we should be able to achieve the same level of professional success as a man based on our talents and abilities—and not on our appearance or our sexual prowess. On the other hand, Alvaré says, we actually cooperate and even encourage our own objectification to the point of going to great length in some cases to hide what we should be holding most dear—our ability to bring new life into the world. For example, "in North America, a certain form of cosmetic surgery post-childbirth, going by the name of a 'mommy job,' is performed upon perfectly healthy women thousands of times a year, to erase all of the side effects of pregnancy." [30]

Regarding the treatment of women, the Church has recognized that many changes to address specific areas of discrimination were definitely needed; however, as Alvaré points out, such changes did not require drawing "upon the worst features of male behavior". [31]

A woman's extreme makeover must start first with a cultural detoxification. Bit by bit we have to peel away those layers of faulty messages and wean ourselves off of a certain type of thinking—or in some cases *start* thinking instead of just sitting there absorbing all the junk around us like a lifeless sponge. We need to change our current way of seeing the world, as Matthew Kelly says, because it is affecting everything in that world—the way we live our lives and, more important, our relationship with God and one another.

[30] Helen Alvaré, "The Reduction of Femininity to an Object of Consumerism" (International Convention on the Theme "Woman and Man, the *Humanum* in Its Entirety", Vatican City, February 8, 2008).

[31] Ibid.

I once thought myself to be a pretty astute woman. However, I slowly learned just how much I didn't know and just how much I was actually being betrayed—and how much women in general were, and still are, betrayed by the voices and sources they were led to trust. So what is the truth about who we are as women? Where can that truth be found? I think that deep down in our heart of hearts, we already know the answer. The truth is a person, Jesus Christ. The fullness of *that* truth is found in the Catholic Church. Just as Prego spaghetti sauce claims, "It's all in there." Read on and see what I mean.

Questions for Reflection

1. How much time do you spend with various forms of media?

2. How do you think the mass media may have formed your thinking regarding women's roles in the Church and in society?

3. What types of sources do you consult when making moral decisions, especially when it comes to issues involving intrinsic evils such as abortion, contraception, and euthanasia?

4. How do you think secular media may have impacted your religious practices and beliefs?

5. Do you or your children have a television or a computer in the bedroom?

6. Have you established media guidelines for yourself or your family?

7. Do you see a need to establish media guidelines? If not, why not?

Chapter 3

The Abortion Distortion

Media Falsehoods and the
Fallout That Followed

In a time of universal deceit, telling the truth
becomes a revolutionary act.

— George Orwell

Abortion is supposed to be all about "choice". How many times have you heard—or maybe even said yourself—concerning the abortion debate, "A woman has a right to choose" or "It's my body, my choice"? Such phrases are plastered on posters and banners at proabortion rallics. It's common language when abortion is part of a news report or appears in a story line in a feature film or a prime-time program: choice, choice, choice! "Choice" and "right to choose" have become catch-all sayings anywhere abortion is discussed, including college campuses, hospitals, doctor's offices, and medical schools. There has been an ongoing effort to condition the general public to accept this idea that a woman should be—and is—free to "choose" whether to end the life growing inside her. Several culprits have been collaborating in this very damaging campaign. Based on the research I presented in the last chapter, in which I outlined the general attitude of the media regarding Christianity, abortion, and sex, it should come as no surprise that the media is at the top of the partners-in-crime list, which also includes politicians, university professors, medical professionals, and activists. Sad to say that plenty of clerical and lay Catholic leaders, who ought to know better, also belong to this group.

Common sense tells us that having a choice is not the same thing as making a good choice. When it comes to having an abortion, however, choice has little to do with it. Discovering this truth was eye-opening and life-changing for me, especially as someone who had spent her career as a reporter and investigator. I was shocked to learn how abortion advocates—with the help of the mass media—distort and deny the facts about abortion to the detriment of women, all the while hiding behind a slogan of "choice" or "reproductive freedom".

Let's take a look at a few statistics in one study, *Forced Abortion in America*, conducted by the Elliot Institute:[1]

- 64 percent of women questioned reported feeling pressured to abort.
- 79 percent weren't told of available resources.
- 67 percent weren't counseled before their abortion.
- Most felt rushed or uncertain about their decision.
- The clinics involved failed to screen for coercion.

This is what "choice" *really* looks like in our culture.

The Abortion Propaganda Machine

How did the "pro-choice" term become so universally accepted to begin with? A quick check on the Merriam-Webster

[1] Elliot Institute, *Forced Abortion in America: A Special Report* (2010), http://www.theunchoice.com/pdf/FactSheets/ForcedAbortions.pdf.

website says that the first known use of the term was way back in 1975. *Pro-choice* is defined as "favoring the legalization of abortion". So why can't abortion supporters just be up-front and say that? Why do they always use the euphemism "choice"? For the same reason that abortion supporters invented the phrase in the first place: the reality of abortion is ugly, and people inherently don't want to be associated with something so abhorrent.

As the late physician Bernard Nathanson, one of the original founders of NARAL, has stated in numerous interviews, he and other leaders in NARAL greatly deceived the American public on the issues of abortion in a push to get it legalized and deemed morally acceptable to the public.

> We claimed that between five and ten thousand women a year died of botched abortions. The actual figure was closer to 200 to 300 and we also claimed that there were a million illegal abortions a year in the United States and the actual figure was close to 200,000. So we were guilty of massive deception.
>
> As a founding member and chairman of the medical committee, I accepted the figures which came from a biostatistician name Christopher Tietze and he and his wife passed along these figures to us at NARAL. We were in no position to validate them or not, so we accepted them in the interest of higher standards, or at least higher objectives.[2]

Nathanson eventually not only left his abortion practice behind, but became a staunch pro-life advocate and eventually converted to Catholicism. He died in February 2011 after a prolonged battle with cancer. He was eighty-four years old.

[2] Bernard Nathanson interview by Spider Jones, *CFRB Talk Show*, July 9, 2008, cited in "Former Abortionist Bernard Nathanson Exposes Lies of American Pro-Abortion Movement", LifeSiteNews.com, July 29, 2008, www.lifesitenews.com/news/archive/ldn/2008/jul/08072904.

Researchers say that the money behind what is now a billion-dollar industry is a driving force as big as, or even bigger than, the radical feminist ideology that sparked the original abortion battle. Among these researchers is Vicki Evans, the Respect Life coordinator for the Archdiocese of San Francisco. In her 2009 report *Commercial Markets Created by Abortion: Profiting from the Fetal Distribution Chain*, Evans outlines how Planned Parenthood Federation of America (PPFA), the number one abortion provider in the country, achieved the status of a billion-dollar industry. Between 2003 and 2008, PPFA saw abortion expand from an $810 million business to a $1.038 billion industry, surpassing the billion-dollar revenue mark in the 2006–2007 fiscal year.[3] Evans claims that PPFA brings in some of that money through clinical trials conducted with pharmaceutical companies to develop new contraceptives. "Thirty percent of its [PPFA's] clinical trials included teens, age[s] thirteen to eighteen. Attracting teenagers to contraceptive use is a component of the abortion industry's business plan, as is offering abortion as a remedy for failed birth control."[4] In other words, PPFA encourages contraceptive use among teens in order to increase their sexual activity and therefore the number of abortions performed—and abortion is where the real profit lies.

Evans looked at the growing market for abortion-related products and the businesses that provide them. These

[3] Peter J. Smith, "New Study 'Follows the Money' of Abortion", LifeSite News.com, May 7, 2010, http://www.lifesitenews.com/news/archive/ldn/2010/may/10050711; Victoria Evans, *Commercial Markets Created by Abortion: Profiting from the Fetal Distribution Chain* (dissertation for the licentiate in bioethics, Athenaeum Pontificium Regina Apostolorum, November 18, 2009), p. 15. https//o.b5z.net/i/u/10060511/f/Licentiate_Thesis_PDF1.pdf.

[4] Evans, *Commercial Markets Created by Abortion*, p. 19.

companies use aborted fetal material in certain medical treatments and in cosmetic procedures. With a vested interest in widespread abortion, they lobby against attempts to outlaw or regulate it. "It's important to shine a light on these practices that take place behind closed doors. There are powerful forces conspiring to keep this information from the public and the media with the ostensible conviction that they are protecting a woman's right to choose." [5]

Unfortunately, the news media, as the research indicates, is not even slightly interested in coming clean on the abortion distortion. They should be treating this story as one of the biggest cover-ups of the last forty years.

Evans' report is a fascinating look at the money trail. She also raises some very thought-provoking questions for Mr. and Mrs. John Q. Public:

> Is there a commercial case for preserving the abortion industry in its present form that transcends ideology? Are special interests driving the industry? How much power, if any, do financial considerations wield when weighed against societal norms, rules, and laws that govern abortion? Does the public's ignorance of these factors contribute to maintaining the abortion culture as it exists today? If people understood these factors, might their ideas about abortion change? [6]

The general public is ignorant of the financial motivation behind the abortion propaganda machine. I host a daily talk show on the EWTN Global Catholic Radio Network, and while this audience is better informed than most, I still receive numerous e-mails from listeners who are stunned to learn that propping up the "keep abortion legal" signs is a huge, lucrative industry.

[5] Ibid., p. 66.
[6] Ibid., p. 5.

"Safe, Legal, and Rare"

Let's stop and think about one very popular phrase, mentioned in the previous chapter: "Abortion should be safe, legal, and rare." Thanks, but no thanks, Mr. President—as in former president Bill Clinton. He began using the phrase in the early nineties, and those who have bought into it are in need of a major reality check.

Safe

We'll start with the "safe" part of the equation. Despite what certain politicians, the media, and other abortion proponents have told us since *Roe v. Wade*, abortion is not a minor or always-safe medical procedure that benefits women. We've already established the fact that many women don't really "choose" abortion but often feel pressured or forced into the decision. Now we will go into more detail concerning how and why abortion, instead of being safe, is in actuality a procedure that can place women in harm's way. This is due to emotional complications, domestic situations (often involving violence suffered at the hands of a spouse, relative, or boyfriend, who pressures the woman to have an abortion), and last—but certainly not least—serious health problems from the actual abortion itself.

There are a number of organizations, ministries, psychologists, researchers, and medical doctors who have been researching the emotional and physical impact of abortion. Due to the proabortion agenda prevalent in today's culture, it is often difficult for these researchers to get their material recognized in prominent medical journals and other outlets that receive attention. That is why I want to shine a light on the work of these brave souls who are trying to provide as much information as possible to abortion-minded women.

Despite what NARAL/Pro-Choice America, Planned Parenthood, EMILY's List, and others say, abortion is not good for women. For example:

- More than 30 studies between 2005 and 2010 show the negative impact of abortion on women.[7]
- 65 percent of post-abortive American women were found to have multiple symptoms of post-traumatic stress disorder.[8]
- Substance abuse is 4.5 times higher among women with past abortions.[9]
- Illegal drug use is 6.1 times higher among women with history of abortion compared to women with no history of abortion.[10]
- Post-abortive women in Finland had a 650 percent higher risk of death from suicide compared to women who carried to term.[11]

Now, unless you have been sequestered underground or in a backwoods cave somewhere, you have certainly seen the high-profile campaigns dedicated to raising awareness of breast cancer. The American Cancer Society says that

[7] Priscilla Coleman, "Thirty Studies in Five Years Show Abortion Hurts Women's Mental Health", LifeNews.com, November 12, 2010, www.lifenews.com/2010/11/12/opi-1006/.

[8] Martha Shuping, M.D., "Posttraumatic Stress Disorder After Abortion," www.rachelnetwork.org/images/Posttraumatic_Stress_Disorder_After_Abortion.pdf.

[9] David C. Reardon and Phillip G. Ney, "Abortion and Drug Abuse", *American Journal of Drug & Alcohol Abuse* 26, no. 1, (February 2000):61–75.

[10] Kazvo Yamagachi and Denise Kandel, "Drug Use and Other Determinants of Premarital Pregnancy and Its Outcome: A Dynamic Analysis of Competing Life Events", *Journal of Marriage and the Family* 49 (May 1987): 257–70.

[11] Martha Shuping, M.D., "Deaths Associated with Abortion and Childbirth: A Brief Summary with Attention to Mental Health Issues", www.rachelnetwork.org/images/Deaths_Associated_with_Abortion_and_Childbirth.pdf.

breast cancer is the second leading cause of death in women (following lung cancer) and is the most common cancer among women, excluding certain types of skin cancer. But did you know that even one abortion doubles a woman's risk of developing breast cancer, and that that risk increases further with two or more abortions?[12]

This connection deserves some serious attention because of the sheer numbers involved. A study released on May 23, 2011, by the Guttmacher Institute (the research arm of Planned Parenthood) "estimates that given the current abortion rate, nearly one in 10 U.S. women of reproductive age will have an abortion by age 20, one-quarter by age 30 and nearly one-third by age 45."[13] There are, on average, about one million abortions a year in this country. These are staggering numbers. This is not to say that every woman who develops breast cancer has had an abortion or that the opposite is true. But with the number of abortions so high in this country, with the high rate of breast cancer among women and the evidence of the abortion–breast cancer connection continuing to pile up, why aren't women told of this risk when they walk into an abortion facility?

Each year, we are encouraged to "think pink". When National Breast Cancer Awareness Month rolls around in October, there is so much pink in the malls, in magazine advertisements, on websites, and in the grocery stores that it feels like we're living inside a giant bottle of Pepto-Bismol. We need to "rethink the pink" before we pin on

[12] H. L. Howe, R. T. Senie, H. Bzduch, and P. Herzfeld, "Early Abortion and Breast Cancer Risk among Women under Age 40", *International Journal of Epidemiology* 18 (1989): 300–304; cited in Elliot Institute, "Physical Risks".

[13] Guttmacher Institute, "Abortion Rate Increasing among Poor Women, Even as it Decreases among Most Other Groups", May 23, 2011, http://www.guttmacher.org/media/nr/2011/05/23/ab.html.

those ribbons. And before we open our wallets, we need to do a quick background check and follow the money. Each year, hundreds of thousands of women and men put their time, efforts, and well-meaning intentions into Susan G. Komen Race for the Cure events. These are key fundraisers that claim to be targeting breast cancer research. Komen, along with the mass media—which often sponsors or promotes these events—doesn't tell participants about the organization's strong financial support of Planned Parenthood. Remember, Planned Parenthood has the dubious distinction of being the number one abortion provider in the country. Its size is due in part to the money it receives from donations and grants, such as Komen's. (Planned Parenthood also receives a sizable chunk of change from the federal government in terms of our tax dollars. According to the organization STOPP [Stop Planned Parenthood], in 2009 Planned Parenthood received nearly $350 million in tax dollars.[14])

In 2004 Eve Sanchez Silver quit her research position at the Komen foundation because of Komen's support of Planned Parenthood. Silver is a breast cancer survivor who runs her own research organization, Cinta Latina Research, which studies the effects of breast cancer on minorities. In an interview with LifeNews.com, a pro-life news site, Sanchez said that women deserve to know about the abortion-breast cancer link. This is especially important for non-Caucasian women, because for them the risk is even greater than for Caucasian women. "Black and Latina women have very aggressive breast cancers often reported very late, often, unhappily, too late. If there are facts to be

---

[14] Steven Ertelt, "Planned Parenthood Abortion Biz President Makes about $400,000", LifeNews.com, November 11, 2010, http://www.lifenews.com/2010/11/11/nat-6843/.

known they should be broadcasted, not swept under the rug." [15]

Komen denies the link between abortion and breast cancer, even though according to the Coalition on Abortion/Breast Cancer there have been some seventy-two epidemiological studies since 1957, 80 percent of which show the abortion–breast cancer link. [16] You will find a number of good resources on the "ABC link", but Karen Malec, the president and cofounder of the Coalition on Abortion/Breast Cancer, gives a general explanation concerning the increased breast cancer risks for women who have aborted.

> The breasts grow considerably during pregnancy while under the influence of high levels of the hormone estrogen, a known carcinogen. Estrogen causes the woman's normal and cancer-vulnerable breast lobules to multiply. If she has an abortion, she's left with more places for cancers to start in her breasts. If she has a baby, then other pregnancy hormones mature her breast lobules into cancer-resistant lobules during the last months of pregnancy. She's left with more cancer-resistant tissue than she had before she became pregnant. [17]

When I began to look at the compelling evidence for the ABC link, the God factor was so obvious. Life gives life. We were not designed to kill our children. As Malec and other researchers point out, one of the strongest protective factors where breast cancer is concerned is early pregnancy. Each year that a woman delays her first full-term pregnancy increases her risk for breast cancer.

[15] Steven Ertelt, "Former Komen Breast Cancer Advisor Speaks Out on Abortion Link", LifeNews.com, January 13, 2005, http://www.lifenews.com/2005/01/13/nat-1107/.

[16] Karen Malec, "The ABC [Abortion–Breast Cancer] Link", Coalition on Abortion/Breast Cancer, http://www.abortionbreastcancer.com/The_Link.htm.

[17] Ibid.

There is a natural order in terms of the way our bodies are designed. When we go against that plan, we make a mess of things for ourselves, and the mess spills over into our families—and into society. We can see this fallout not only in terms of abortion's physical effects on women but also in terms of its psychological effects. A study conducted by researchers at the University of Manitoba and published in the April 2010 issue of the *Canadian Journal of Psychiatry* showed that women who undergo abortions are nearly four times as likely to experience problems with drugs and alcohol compared to women who have not had abortions.[18] The study also found "connections between abortion and other mental health conditions like mood disorders, but substance use disorders showed the strongest link".[19]

Legal

Before Roe v. Wade, abortion advocates argued that legal abortions would be safe because they would be guided by the regulations and laws that apply to other surgical procedures. Since abortion was made a constitutional right, however, abortionists have become a protected group; as a result, some have been able to violate health standards with impunity.

In January 2011, the gruesome story about Philadelphia abortionist Kermit Gosnell exemplified just how out of control the abortion industry has become. Gosnell was charged with seven counts of murder for allegedly killing babies who were born alive. He was also charged with murder for giving

[18] Natalie P. Mota, Margaret Burnett, and Jitender Sareen, "Associations between Abortion, Mental Disorders, and Suicidal Behaviour in a Nationally Representative Sample", *Canadian Journal of Psychiatry* 55, no. 4 (April 2010): 239–47, http://publications.cpa-apc.org/media.php?mid=951.

[19] Paul Turenne, "Study Links Abortion and Addiction", *Toronto Sun*, May 1, 2010, http://www.torontosun.com/news/canada/2010/05/01/13790291.html.

a lethal dose of Demerol to one of his patients. But the shocking allegations don't stop there. Reading the following findings of the Grand Jury, it is easy to see why Philadelphia police referred to Gosnell's facility as a "house of horrors" and why prosecutors called the West Philadelphia Women's Medical Society as a "baby Charnel house":

- Gosnell regularly and illegally delivered live, viable babies in the third trimester and then murdered these newborns by severing their spinal cords with scissors.
- Conditions at the clinic were unsanitary. Cats were allowed to roam and defecate freely. The furniture and blankets were bloodstained. Instruments and medical equipment were not sterilized. Disposable items were used more than once. Fetal remains were stored in jars, bags and plastic jugs all over the facility.
- Fundamental safety measures were ignored. Vital pieces of equipment were broken. The emergency exit was padlocked shut. A janitor testified that the bathrooms were cleaned just once a week, even though patients routinely vomited into sinks and miscarried into toilets.
- Even though accusations against Gosnell had been made before the January 2011 arrests, they were ignored by those responsible for oversight. While the National Abortion Federation refused Gosnell's application for membership because of the deplorable conditions in his clinic, the organization failed to report him to authorities.[20]

This story made international headlines, but unfortunately only for a short time because the media chose to

[20] Section One Overview, Report of the Grand Jury, R. Seth Williams District Attorney First Judicial District of Pennsylvania.

treat the case as an anomaly. If this were any other medical procedure in the spotlight, we would no doubt still be hearing and reading about it. Reporters would have investigated the employees involved to see if they were connected to other medical facilities around the country. They would have looked at other abortion clinics to see if illegal and life-threatening activities were unique to Gosnell or occurring elsewhere.

If the media were doing its job, it would see a pattern of misconduct in the abortion industry. In the last two years, abortion clinics in New Jersey, Alabama, California, Louisiana, Michigan, Maryland, and Kansas, just to name a few, have been investigated for violations of health care regulations, unreported cases of statutory rape, and problems with the licenses—or lack thereof—of the abortionists themselves.

- In Kansas a case against a Planned Parenthood facility involving 107 criminal charges, including 23 felonies, was remanded to the state's highest court.[21]
- Officials in New Jersey accused an abortionist, already under close scrutiny in three other states, of putting women at additional risk through botched abortions.[22]
- In Alabama the health department found violations at a Planned Parenthood abortion facility regarding the state's parental consent law.[23]

---

[21] "Maryland Considers Banning Interstate Abortions in Light of Case of N.J. Doctor", Associated Press, January 14, 2011, www.nj.com/news/index.ssf/2011/01/maryland_considers_banning_int.html.

[22] "Pro-Life Victory: KS Supreme Court Allows Planned Parenthood Criminal Case to Go Forward", Operation Rescue, October 15, 2010, www.operationrescue.org/archives/pro-life-victory-ks-supreme-court-allows-planned-parenthood-criminal-case-to-go-forward/.

[23] Steven Ertelt, "Document Reveals More Abortion, Sexual Abuse Violations at Planned Parenthood", LifeNews.com, February 16, 2010, www.lifenews.com/2010/02/16/state-4815/.

This is the stuff of investigative journalism and Pulitzer prizes, but because the malfeasance involves the sacred cow of abortion, the mass media remains silent. Those trying to break through this wall of silence are, for the most part, media savvy, young pro-life activists. The most well-known is Lila Rose, founder of Live Action. In early 2011, investigative reporters from Live Action posed as sex traffickers and visited Planned Parenthood offices in New Jersey, Virginia, Washington, D.C., and New York. The disguised reporters inquired about getting contraceptives and abortions for underage sex workers. In their role planning, they openly discussed the exploitation of minors. The Planned Parenthood staffers not only failed to report these supposed sex traffickers to the authorities, as they are required to do by law, but they also counseled the pimps on how to work the system if they don't have health insurance.

Planned Parenthood has denied it has broken the law, but it has changed more than once its explanation of the unlawful behavior of its staff. In a February 2011 press release, Live Action President Lila Rose said Planned Parenthood is unable to defend itself. "An institutional crisis has consumed Planned Parenthood at the highest levels. The reason their story has changed five times in reaction to our investigation is because they know they are guilty."[24]

The abortion business has been duplicitous from the beginning. Even the United States Supreme Court cases that made abortion a constitutional right were built on lies. Abortion proponents consider *Roe v. Wade* the landmark case that turned the abortion tide in their favor back in 1973. They're correct about the impact it had. Did you ever wonder,

---

[24] David Schmidt, "DC Planned Parenthood Staffer Counsels Sex-Trafficker How Underage Girls Can Get Abortions and Testing, No Questions Asked", Liveaction.org, February 10, 2011, www.liveaction.org/blog/dc-planned-parenthood-sex-trafficker/.

then—since the case is so important to so many supporting legalized abortion—why we don't see the Jane Roe of *Roe v. Wade* out there promoting abortion and doing Planned Parenthood commercials? Who is she, and where is she?

Jane Roe's real name is Norma McCorvey. She is well known in the pro-life movement but not to the general public; unfortunately, a number of Catholics and other concerned Christians also are not familiar with her story and how the proabortion machine quickly pushed her aside when they felt she would not or could not benefit their cause any longer. McCorvey never actually even had an abortion. As McCorvey describes in her many talks and in her 1997 biography, *Won by Love*, she was "poor, pregnant, and desperate and fell into the hands of ambitious lawyers".[25] The attorneys were looking for someone to help them challenge prohibitive abortion laws in Texas. McCorvey agreed to help them with their cause and signed the papers making her the plaintiff in the case that would result in legalized abortion on demand in the entire nation. Through her Roe No More ministry, she has shared openly at many a pro-life rally and fundraiser that she told blatant lies to help the lawsuit against Texas move forward, including claiming that she had been gang-raped.

McCorvy has long been public about her own difficult journey to Christianity and her eventual conversion to the Catholic Church, a story that briefly made the secular headlines. In her book, she also details her battles with drugs, alcohol, and suicide attempts, which were the result of learning the role Jane Roe actually played in legalizing abortion. McCorvey recounts that once she had served the lawyers'

---

[25] Norma McCorvey, with Gary Thomas, *Won by Love: Norma McCorvey, Jane Roe of Roe v. Wade, Speaks Out for the Unborn as She Shares Her New Conviction for Life* (Nashville: T. Nelson Publishers, 1997), inside cover.

purpose, she was tossed aside, because an uneducated and unskilled woman with substance abuse issues didn't exactly fit the feminist image of the day. McCorvey, who spent twenty-eight years working at abortion clinics, also gives a detailed insider's look at the ugliness of the abortion business. Today, in addition to her activities on the pro-life speaking circuit, McCorvey also works closely with pregnancy resource centers and other pro-life organizations, including the Justice Foundation, Priests for Life, and the Silent No More Awareness Campaign. In 2003 McCorvey filed a motion to reopen the original case and request that it be overturned, but the motion was denied by the U.S. Court of Appeals. I wonder how many people, especially those who call themselves "pro-choice", know the real story about Jane Roe?

Next up, does the Supreme Court case *Doe v. Bolton*, or the name Sandra Cano, ring any bells? Sandra Cano was the Mary Doe in *Doe v. Bolton*, the less well-known companion case to *Roe v. Wade*. Like Norma McCorvey, Sandra Cano never had an abortion, and she too is a pro-life speaker and activist. As Cano explains in her testimony, which is detailed at her Wonderfully Made Ministry website (www.wonderfullymadeministry.com), she never even testified in the case. Cano was pregnant when she went to a legal aid agency in connection with her divorce and child custody case. She never sought or wanted an abortion but later realized abortion was the issue for her attorney. Her case created the health exception that allows abortion up to the very day of birth. She struggled for years to get the court records of her case unsealed. In 2003 she filed a motion to reverse *Doe v. Bolton*, but the U.S. Supreme Court declined to reopen the case.

> It took me until 1988 to get my records unsealed in order for me to try and find the answer to those questions and to join in the movement to stop abortion in America. When

proabortion advocates found out about my efforts, my car was vandalized on one occasion and at another time, someone shot at me while I was on my front porch holding my grandbaby. I am angry. I feel like my name, life, and identity have been stolen and put on this case without my knowledge and against my wishes. How dare they use my name and my life this way![26]

Rare

Last but not least, let's focus on the "rare" portion of Clinton's statement. "Rare" equals nearly fifty million abortions over about forty years. Going back to the figure of one million abortions annually, would anyone associate the word *rare* with that seven-digit number? Try getting your brain around those statistics—and those are the numbers just for the United States! Using the word *rare* in terms of abortion numbers is also an incredible insult to the African American and Hispanic American communities. African Americans make up 12 percent of the population in our country, but according to the Guttmacher Institute, 30 percent of the abortions nationwide are performed on black women, and 25 percent are performed on Hispanic women.[27]

The targeting of minorities, especially the African American community, can be traced to the origins of Planned Parenthood and its founder, Margaret Sanger. Current Planned Parenthood promoters try to dispute Sanger's eugenics history or to distance themselves from her original ideas of sterilization for those seen as "unfit"—which included

[26] Sandra Cano, testimony, "The Consequences of *Roe v. Wade* and *Doe v. Bolton*", United States Senate Committee on the Judiciary, June 23, 2005, http://judiciary.senate.gov/hearings/testimony.cfm?id=e655f9e2809e5476862f735da107c92d&wit_id=e655f9e2809e5476862f735da107c92d-1-1.

[27] Guttmacher Institute, *Facts on Induced Abortion in the United States*, May 2011, www.guttmacher.org/pubs/fb_induced_abortion.html.

African Americans.[28] Disputing, dismissing, or denying what Margaret Sanger and her Planned Parenthood was, and is, all about is getting more and more difficult given the sheer number of abortions performed on minorities as well as the fact that many an abortion center is located where large minority populations reside. If we think this is mere coincidence, then I suggest we all start looking for oceanfront property in Arizona.

For many years, organizations such as the American Life League's STOPP International (www.stopp.org) and www.blackgenocide.org have been researching and documenting the pro-eugenics agenda of Planned Parenthood and its founder, Margaret Sanger. In the documentary "MAAFA 21", well-known pro-life activist and undercover investigator Mark Crutcher of Life Dynamics details the history of Planned Parenthood's original agenda, which is still being played out in the twenty-first century. Sanger was quoted in a 1925 *New York Times* article following her appearance at an international conference on birth control:

> While the United States shuts her gates to foreigners, no attempt is made to discourage the rapid multiplication of undesirable aliens—and natives—within our own borders. On the contrary the United States deliberately encourages, and even makes necessary by its laws, the breeding, with a breakneck rapidity, of idiots, defectives, diseased, feeble-minded and criminal classes. The American public is too heavily taxed to maintain an increasing race of morons which threatens the very foundation of our civilization.[29]

[28] "The Truth About Margaret Sanger: How Planned Parenthood Duped America", *Citizen Magazine*, January 20, 1992, www.blackgenocide.org/sanger.html.

[29] *The New York Times* Archives, "Conference Opens on Birth Control: Sanger Says 'Undesirables Are Increasing in Population' ", March 26, 1925, http://www.freerepublic.com/focus/f-news/1399004/posts.

Denying the Truth about Abortion

The evidence presented above, which I should stress just scratches the surface of abortion and only begins to open its ugly can of worms, brings the entire notion of "safe, legal, and rare" into serious question, doesn't it? The research points to the beauty and the accuracy of Church teaching. If abortion is such a good thing, then why is there so much misery and pain attached to it?

Abortion and other attacks on the human person are associated with a misguided understanding of freedom and have set off a negative chain reaction in society, as Pope John Paul II explained in *Evangelium Vitae* (*The Gospel of Life*).

> This view of freedom leads to a serious distortion of life in society. If the promotion of the self is understood in terms of absolute autonomy, people inevitably reach the point of rejecting one another. Everyone else is considered an enemy from whom one has to defend oneself. Thus society becomes a mass of individuals placed side by side, but without any mutual bonds. Each one wishes to assert himself independently of the other and in fact intends to make his own interests prevail. Still, in the face of other people's analogous interests, some kind of compromise must be found, if one wants a society in which the maximum possible freedom is guaranteed to each individual. In this way, any reference to common values and to a truth absolutely binding on everyone is lost, and social life ventures on to the shifting sands of complete relativism. At that point, everything is negotiable, everything is open to bargaining: even the first of the fundamental rights, the right to life.[30]

[30] *Evangelium Vitae* (March 25, 1995), 20, Holy See website, http://www.vatican.va/holy_father/john_paul_ii/encyclicals/documents/hf_jp-ii_enc_25031995_evangelium-vitae_en.html.

Unfortunately, those who want to hang on to the golden calf of abortion have plenty of company and plenty of help promoting their cause. Those who stand on that side of the fence even go so far as to ignore the cries of literally thousands of women (and now men as well) who are speaking out and telling how abortion was not the answer to their problems and in the end only made those problems much worse. How does that kind of denial happen unless you are living in the Twilight Zone? Let's make sure we understand this correctly. Suppose you are with NOW, or NARAL Pro-Choice America, or Planned Parenthood. You are steadfast in your belief that abortion must be legal to guarantee "reproductive freedom". But you don't at least dialogue with women who have had negative and painful experiences with the very thing you're saying is good for them?

Many women—and men—who have been hurt by abortion have joined their voices in the Silent No More Awareness Campaign, a project of Priests for Life and Anglicans for Life. Cofounded by Janet Morana and Georgette Forney, the campaign is a Christian ministry attempting to raise awareness of the "devastation abortion brings to women and men".[31] Actress, model, and author Jennifer O'Neill is the campaign's celebrity spokesperson.

One of the group's most well-known activities is the annual rally on the steps of the United States Supreme Court on January 22, the anniversary of the *Roe v. Wade* decision. At the end of the March for Life in Washington, D.C., post-abortive women and men bravely come forward to talk about their abortion experience and why they are "silent no more". The testimonies are heartbreaking and encouraging at the same time. It is extremely sad to hear how abortion adversely

[31] Silent No More Awareness Campaign, "About Us", http://www.silentnomoreawareness.org/about/index.html#who.

affected people's lives for years and often led to relationship breakdowns, drug and alcohol addictions, psychological trauma, and other problems. It's extremely moving to hear how they were able not only to forgive themselves and turn their own lives around but to help other people as well.

If it weren't for the coverage on EWTN (the Eternal Word Television Network), Christian and conservative talk radio, and C-SPAN, you would not know much about the Silent No More Awareness Campaign or the March for Life, despite the fact that the march is truly massive. The March for Life brings together hundreds of thousands of pro-lifers from around the world—I know because I cover this event each year. In 2011 the crowd was estimated to be over four hundred thousand. Watch any mainstream TV coverage on the event, and you will see nothing but smoke and mirrors. Usually the standard operating procedure for the few outlets that do decide to cover it involves showing close-up images of pro-lifers and their signs or posters and then doing the same with the three dozen or so proabortion activists who show up at the end of the march, near the Silent No More Awareness Campaign gathering. The copy usually reads something like this: "Both sides showed up in the nation's capital today, the anniversary of the Supreme Court decision that led to the legalization of abortion in America."

Both sides? We have hundreds of thousands versus barely a few dozen, and this "both sides" song and dance is sold to the public as an accurate and factual representation of a major event? Such irresponsible coverage is an attempt to convince the public that the pro-life movement is not all that large or active.

Abortion is still an issue at election time and was a key issue during the health care reform debate. Those two factors alone, not to mention the huge turnout year after year at the March for Life, should result in major coverage by local and national media. Meanwhile, abortion advocates, whether they are dressed up as reporters, politicians, lawyers, feminists, college professors, or medical professionals, need to keep tap dancing around the truth or stomping altogether on the facts, figures, studies, and personal testimonies in order to keep their vaudeville act on the road, and in business.

Questions for Reflection

1. Do you consider yourself pro-life or a supporter of legalized abortion?
2. What type of prayer, discernment, and research have you done on the issue of abortion?
3. How much of an influence has the culture and secular media been in determining your opinions on abortion?
4. Did you consult Catholic sources, including the *Catechism of the Catholic Church*[32] (nos. 2270–75) and other Church documents (such as Pope Paul VI, *Humanae Vitae* and Blessed John Paul II, *Evangelium Vitae*) prior to forming your opinion?
5. Were you aware of the pattern of deceptive information marketed through the media regarding abortion?

---

[32] *Catechism of the Catholic Church*, 2nd ed. (Vatican City: Libreria Editrice Vaticana, 1997). All references to the *Catechism* are to this edition.

Chapter 4

"Free Sex" and the Contraception Deception

Bondage Sold as Freedom

Sex is the mysticism of materialism and the only possible religion in a materialistic culture.

— Malcolm Muggeridge

A friend of mine, who is a Catholic moral theologian and a regular guest on my radio show, shared with me and my listeners a sad and quite sobering story regarding the sorry state of our oversexualized culture. She was giving a talk on a college campus concerning God's plan for sexuality. In her presentation, she did her best to encourage the young people to stay chaste, and she emphatically explained that if they had not been living chastely, it was never too late; God allows U-turns. After her seminar, she was approached by an attractive student. The young woman explained how she had no idea that she did *not* have to engage in sexual activity before marriage. This was big, and I mean really big, breaking news to her. This was the first time she was given the "okay", so to speak, to say no. She was under the strong and terribly misguided impression—from her fellow students, her environment, and her life experience in general—that she should have one sexual partner, if not more, at any given time; otherwise, she would be abnormal and treated as an outcast.

Is this the liberation that women fought so hard for just decades ago? Call me crazy, but I thought the bra-burning brigade was after quite the opposite: preventing men from pressuring women into unwanted sex and creating a new world where women would be valued for more than just their bodies, a world where women would be valued for their many unique gifts and talents and would be able to develop these to the same extent as men. So much for progress.

The episode described by my moral theologian friend occurred on an American college campus in 2009, but the feelings expressed by the college student are common among women across the country and around the globe. Many unmarried women assume that their happiness depends upon being in a sexual relationship. And in order to have sex outside of marriage "safely", contraception is absolutely necessary. Contraception has become as commonplace an item on a modern woman's grocery list as toothpaste, deodorant, and a loaf of bread.

The media has played a big role in shaping women's attitudes about sex. By watching hours and hours of television shows and movies, many single women have come to believe that if they're not imitating the lifestyle of the near-nymphomaniac Samantha Jones of *Sex and the City* fame, then they are not, as another one of my good friends likes to say, "all that and a bag of chips". As a matter of fact, they are living in the Dark Ages. They're repressed or oppressed—or both. Letting go and leaping from bed to bed and from relationship to relationship like smart and sex-savvy Sam, on the other hand, is freedom and happiness.

Really? Put quite simply, if jumping from bed to bed and engaging in all kinds of sexual experimentation is so wonderfully grand, so ultimately fulfilling, and so freeing, why is there so much misery and pain attached to it? And why are so many baby boomers and others who spent their youth promoting and practicing "free love" so downright unhappy with their sex lives? According to an October 2010 poll by the Associated Press and LifeGoesStrong.com, a quarter of Americans—24 percent between the ages of forty-five and sixty-five—say they are dissatisfied with their sex lives.[1] And remember good old Dr. Ruth, the well-known sex therapist? Well, she says one of the problems is unmet expectations. Dr. Ruth told Megyn Kelly of Fox News that those expectations come from believing, in part at least, that our lives are supposed to mirror what we see on TV and in the movies, and when we find out that such a lifestyle is not all it's cracked up to be, then disappointment, disillusion, and dissatisfaction set in.[2]

Toxic Culture: The Research

Most of us recognize that the media has been inundated with sex. Few, however, realize the degree to which we are swimming in smut. It doesn't matter whether I am speaking at a Catholic parish or at a parent-teacher night at a public school—audiences are floored by the statistics. An incredible amount of research has been done on the connection between the media and the overall decline in morality. The vast majority of the studies are conducted by secular

[1] "Associated Press–LifeGoesStrong.com Relationships Survey", October 10, 2010, http://surveys.ap.org/data/KnowledgeNetworks/AP_LifeGoesStrong_Relationships_Topline_112210.PDF. See also Ken Baron, "New Poll Reveals That We Are Not Happy with Our Sex Lives", LifeGoesStrong.com, November 22, 2010, http://www.lifegoesstrong.com/sex-poll.

[2] Fox News, *America with Megyn Kelly*, "Baby Boomers Having Bad Sex?", November 23, 2010.

entities and professional organizations, including the American Academy of Pediatrics, the American Psychological Association, the American Medical Association, the Rand Corporation, the Kaiser Family Foundation, and the Pew Research Center for the People and the Press.

Television

When I was growing up in the 1960s and 70s, the sexual revolution had not started to take over the TV air waves. I don't remember too many situation comedies, variety shows, or TV drama series that had my parents concerned about my being exposed to too much sexual or violent content. After all, why would *Here Come the Brides*, starring my then heartthrob Bobby Sherman, or even the popular *Starsky and Hutch* police drama be cause for alarm? Maybe they weren't the most educational or uplifting shows out there, but they certainly pale in comparison to what's on the air waves today and what young people are consuming.

What do you think the Nielsen television ratings service found to be the most popular show among girls ages nine to twelve during a November sweeps period in 2004? It was the not-so-family-friendly show *Desperate Housewives*.[3]

On average, according to the Parents Television Council, young people view at least fourteen thousand sexual messages a year on television.[4] This is due not just to the nature of the content but the amount of time young people spend watching TV. Children often watch TV alone in their bedrooms—which today are basically multimedia centers. Another in-depth report from the Kaiser Family Foundation,

---

[3] "Taming TV: Has Television Gotten Worse?" http://www.parenthood. com/article-topics/taming_tv_has_television_gotten_worse.html/page/2.

[4] "Media Influence on Youth", CrisisConnection.com, http://www. crisisconnectioninc.org/teens/media_influence_on_youth.htm.

Generation M2: Media in the Lives of 8- to 18-Year-Olds, reveals that young people devote, on average, seven hours and thirty-eight minutes a day to using entertainment media.[5] That adds up to more than fifty-three hours a week! That's thirteen hours more a week than most of us spend on the job. This same report revealed that only about three in ten young people say that their parents have given them rules about how much time they may spend watching TV, using the computer, or playing video games.

The Rand Corporation, a nonprofit research group, has shown a connection between the selling of sex on television and an increase in teen pregnancies. A Rand study released in 2008, of two thousand adolescents ages twelve to seventeen, found that teenagers who watch a lot of TV programs with sexual content are more than twice as likely to be involved in a pregnancy.[6] Anita Chandra, a behavioral scientist at Rand and the study's lead author, explains, "Adolescents receive a considerable amount of information about sex through television and that programming typically does not highlight the risks and responsibilities of sex."[7]

In an interview with *USA Today*, Tim Winter, the president of the Parents Television Council, said that this type of programming shouldn't be seen as art or free speech but as something damaging to women. "It's become downright ubiquitous.... Families are under siege, teenage girls are

---

[5] *Generation M2: Media in the Lives of 8- to 18-Year-Olds*, January 2010, http://www.kff.org/entmedia/8010.cfm.

[6] Anita Chandra et al., "Does Watching Sex on Television Predict Teen Pregnancy? Findings from a National Longitudinal Survey of Youth", *Pediatrics* 122 (November 2008): 1047–54, http://pediatrics.aappublications.org/content/122/5/1047.full.html.

[7] Quoted in Shari Roan, "Sexual Content on TV Is Linked to Teen Pregnancy", Booster Shots: Oddities, Musings and News from the Health World, *Los Angeles Times*, November 3, 2008, http://latimesblogs.latimes.com/booster_shots/2008/11/sexual-content.html.

under siege. You don't know what the cultural impact will be down the road." [8]

It's not just the amount of sex on TV that is a problem but the way women are portrayed and treated in story lines. The Parents Television Council, in its report *Women in Peril: A Look at TV's Disturbing New Storyline Trend* (which we mentioned in chapter 2), shows that story lines depicting violence against women are becoming more frequent and sexually graphic "in ways that have not been seen in the history of television".[9] From 2004 to 2009, there was an 81 percent increase in incidents of intimate partner violence on TV. Some of the programs highlighted in the study were *Desperate Housewives, Prison Break, C.S.I.,* and *Medium.*

Music

Music is another troubling source of the "have sex, and lots of it" message. According to a Rand report, teens will become sexually active sooner if they listen to music with sexually degrading lyrics.[10] In 2008 the Parents Television Council outlined how children were being assailed by sex, drugs, violence, and explicit language on cable music channels, including BET (Black Entertainment Television) and MTV.[11] Tim Winter explains that the Parents Television Council found 1,647 instances of offensive or adult content

[8] Gary Strauss, "Sex on TV: It's Increasingly Uncut—and Unavoidable", *USA Today*, January 19, 2010, http://www.usatoday.com/life/television/news/2010-01-20-sexcov20_CV_N.htm.

[9] *Women in Peril: A Look at TV's Disturbing New Storyline Trend*, October 2009, http://www.parentstv.org/PTC/publications/reports/womeninperil/study.pdf.

[10] Steven Martino et al., "Exposure to Degrading Versus Nondegrading Music Lyrics and Sexual Behavior Among Youth", *Pediatrics*, 118, no. 2 (August 2006): E.430–41.

[11] "The Rap on Rap", April 2008, http://www.parentstv.org/ptc/publications/reports/RapStudy/RapStudy.pdf.

in the 27.5 hours of programming analyzed for the study. "BET and MTV are assaulting children with content that is full of sexually charged images, explicit language, portrayals of violence, drug use, drug sales and other illegal activity."[12]

The Internet

When it comes to the Internet and the topic of Internet porn, most people assume the problem is most prevalent among men. But according to a July 2010 article in the conservative publication *The Washington Times*, that's no longer the case. Writer Rachel B. Duke took a look at some of the surveys and found that women now have the dubious distinction of also suffering from the same problem as men and more frequently than one might think.

> Researchers have long known that the Internet has contributed to pornography addiction by making it so easily accessible—no need to go out in a raincoat, pull a hat down over the face, and sneak furtively into the red light district. But that ease of access has leveled the playing field between the sexes—men are known as the sexual risk takers after all—and psychologists and researchers have seen an increasing number of women becoming addicted to pornography on the Internet over the past 10 years. . . .
>
> Psychologists and researchers attribute the increase to the Internet's anonymity and safety. Now a woman needn't sneak into the places good girls avoid.[13]

[12] Parents Television Council, "Children Assaulted by Sex, Violence, Drugs and Explicit Language on BET and MTV", news release, April 10, 2008, http://www.parentstv.org/ptc/news/release/2008/0410.asp.

[13] Rachel B. Duke, "More Women Lured to Pornography Addiction", *Washington Times*, July 11, 2010, http://www.washingtontimes.com/news/2010/jul/11/more-women-lured-to-pornography-addiction.

Cell Phone Texting and "Sexting"

Even something as apparently useful in the right circumstances, such as texting, can be cause for concern in our sex-saturated culture. In 2010, researchers at Case Western Reserve University School of Medicine released a study showing a connection between compulsive texting, or "hypertexting", and risky behavior, including excessive drinking and early sexual activity, among teens. The term *hypertexter* was coined by the researchers to describe someone who sends 120 or more texts per school day. Compared to those who sent fewer texts per day, the hypertexters were nearly three and half times as likely to have sex and 90 percent more likely to report having had more than four sexual partners. Physician Scott Frank, director of the School of Medicine Master of Public Health program at Case Western Reserve, was the lead researcher on the study. "The startling results of this study suggest that when left unchecked texting and other widely popular methods of staying connected are associated with unhealthy behaviors among teenagers.... This may be a wake-up call for parents to open dialogue with their kids about the extent of texting and social networking they are involved with and about what is happening in the rest of their lives." [14]

According to the National Campaign to Prevent Teen and Unplanned Pregnancy, about one in five teens is involved in "sexting", which is the sending of seminude or nude images of themselves over the Internet, usually via a cell phone. [15]

[14] "Hyper-Texting and Hyper-Networking Pose New Health Risks for Teens", Case Western Reserve University News Center, November 10, 2010, http://blog.case.edu/case-news/2010/11/10/hypertexting_and_hypernet working_pose_new_health_risks_for_teens.

[15] National Campaign to Prevent Teen and Unplanned Pregnancy, "Sex and Tech: Results from a Survey of Teens and Young Adults", May 2010, http://www.thenationalcampaign.org/sextech/pdf/sextech_summary.pdf.

Social Networking

We can't ignore the impact of the social networking explosion. In late 2010 there were more than five hundred million active users on Facebook alone. Social networking, while an excellent tool for communication and outreach, poses some very serious issues. In addition to the seemingly endless headlines about online bullying and online sexual predators, more and more reports are surfacing about social networking being connected to a rise in divorce and marital troubles in general. In 2010 the American Academy of Matrimonial Lawyers stated that some 81 percent of its members had "used or faced evidence plucked from Facebook, MySpace, Twitter and other social networking sites, including YouTube and LinkedIn, over the past five years".[16] In 2008 the Pew Internet and American Life Project reported that about one in five adults uses Facebook for flirting.[17]

Some Christian leaders are expressing concern over the impact of social networking on marital fidelity. In 2010 a New Jersey pastor required all married church officials to delete their Facebook accounts because of marital troubles in his church.[18] Other pastors interviewed in the same Associated Press story expressed concern over seeing marriage breakups related to connections made with a past flame via social networking.

[16] Leanne Italie, "Divorce Lawyers Cite Facebook in Evidence", *Fort Wayne Journal Gazette*, September 19, 2010, http://www.journalgazette.net/article/20100919/FEAT/309199992/-1/FEAT11.

[17] Pew Internet and American Life Project, "Social Networks Grow: Friending Mom and Dad", January 2009, http://pewresearch.org/pubs/1079/social-networks-grow.

[18] Audrey Barrick, "New Jersey Pastor Tells Leaders to Get Off Facebook", *The Christian Post*, November 18, 2010, www.christianpost.com/news/nj-pastor-tells-church-leaders-to-get-off-facebook-47694.

Christians and Contraception Don't Mix

There are a plethora of surveys, reports, commentaries, and statistics one could cite on the culture and its connections with sexual promiscuity. Hopefully, you're getting the big picture here: the culture is selling sex as a must-have-and-without-limits commodity. If we must have sex on demand, we must have contraception in order to meet that demand. And following on the heels of contraception is abortion, the back-up plan when contraception fails. Thanks to the combination of radical feminism, decades of abysmal catechesis, and the massive media marketing of sex, women have, by and large, bought into the demand for unlimited sex, contraception, and abortion, and sadly they are the ones suffering the most severe consequences of these behaviors.

In 1968 Pope Paul VI issued his encyclical letter *Humanae Vitae* (*Of Human Life*, subtitled *On the Regulation of Birth*), which reexplained the Church's teaching on birth control. The document was released during what I have called the perfect cultural storm of the mass media explosion and the sexual revolution. Many Church leaders in the United States and elsewhere openly dissented from the Church's ban on contraception, and as a result, many Catholics were told to "follow their conscience" in this matter.

But were they instructed as to what following one's conscience requires? Our conscience needs to be well formed before we make moral decisions. That does not mean reading an article, watching a newscast, or consulting our emotions and then coming to a final conclusion about an important moral question. According to the Church, having a well-formed conscience means we make judgments in "accordance with reason and the divine law".[19] We are

---

[19] *Catechism of the Catholic Church*, no. 1786.

also called to follow the "authoritative" teachings of the Church: "In the formation of conscience the Word of God is the light for our path; we must assimilate it in faith and prayer and put it into practice. We must also examine our conscience before the Lord's Cross. We are assisted by the gifts of the Holy Spirit, aided by the witness or advice of others and guided by the authoritative teaching of the Church." [20]

I used to be one of those Catholics who gave little thought to birth control. As I outlined in my testimony book *Newsflash! My Surprising Journey from Secular Anchor to Media Evangelist,*[21] my husband and I, as we prepared for marriage, were not given any information regarding contraception or Natural Family Planning, a method of birth control approved by the Church because it does not block human fertility. We were merely asked by our pastor, during one of only a very few before-wedding-day meetings, whether we were going to raise our children in the Catholic Church. We cannot blame the pastor, however. We shared in the culpability because we knew, in general, what the Church taught concerning contraception but did nothing to investigate the reasoning behind the teaching. That was a big mistake on our part. Our selfish attitude in the bedroom led to conflicts in other areas of our marriage and a near breakdown of our relationship. Our marriage turned into a record-keeping of who did what to whom and who didn't do enough for whom, but until we made our way back to the Church, we didn't realize the effect contraception was having on our lives.

I know firsthand that the Church is spot-on when she says contraception is a barricade to true intimacy and openness between spouses and between them and God. By using

---

[20] Ibid., no. 1785.

[21] Teresa Tomeo, *Newsflash! My Surprising Journey from Secular Anchor to Media Evangelist* (Waterford, Mich.: Bezalel Books, 2008).

contraception, by blocking their fertility, spouses hold part of themselves back from each other. By separating marital love from the possibility of procreation, they reduce sexual intimacy to pleasure. Using contraception adds to the quid pro quo "I'll do this for you if you'll do that for me" mindset in marriage, which then becomes more like a contractual relationship than one based on God's covenant of the two becoming one in Him. In the words of *Humanae Vitae*:

> To use this divine gift [of sexual intimacy] while depriving it, even if only partially, of its meaning and purpose, is equally repugnant to the nature of man and of woman, and is consequently in opposition to the plan of God and His holy will. But to experience the gift of married love while respecting the laws of conception is to acknowledge that one is not the master of the sources of life but rather the minister of the design established by the Creator.[22]

The Fallout from Contraception

Most people aren't aware that all Christian churches once taught that contraception was wrong. That was up until 1930, when the Anglican church, during its seventh Lambeth Conference, approved contraceptive usage in limited circumstances. Experts on contraception can easily point to the advent of the birth control pill as the catalyst for a stark increase in other major social ills, including sexual promiscuity, sexually transmitted diseases, divorce, abortion, out-of-wedlock births, and poverty, especially among single women.

Could it be that the Church—as in God—was right about contraception all along? Or is the change in the sexual

[22] Paul VI, *Humanae Vitae* (July 25, 1968), 13, Holy See website, http://www.vatican.va/holy_father/paul_vi/encyclicals/documents/hf_p-vi_enc_25071968_humanae-vitae_en.html.

landscape since the wide acceptance of contraception just a coincidence? Some clear answers can be found in the words of Pope Paul VI, who made some very accurate predictions in 1968. In *Humanae Vitae*, he said that four major societal developments would come to pass if contraception were made widely available: (1) there would be a general lowering of morality; (2) respect for women would dramatically decrease; (3) governments would adopt coercive population control policies; and (4) we would "lose reverence due to the whole human organism and its natural functions".[23]

> Responsible men can become more deeply convinced of the truth of the doctrine laid down by the Church on this issue if they reflect on the consequences of methods and plans for artificial birth control. Let them first consider how easily this course of action could open wide the way for marital infidelity and a general lowering of moral standards. Not much experience is needed to be fully aware of human weakness and to understand that human beings—and especially the young, who are so exposed to temptation—need incentives to keep the moral law, and it is an evil thing to make it easy for them to break that law. Another effect that gives cause for alarm is that a man who grows accustomed to the use of contraceptive methods may forget the reverence due to a woman, and, disregarding her physical and emotional equilibrium, reduce her to being a mere instrument for the satisfaction of his own desires, no longer considering her as his partner whom he should surround with care and affection.
>
> Finally, careful consideration should be given to the danger of this power passing into the hands of those public authorities who care little for the precepts of the moral law. Who will blame a government which in its attempt to resolve the problems affecting an entire country resorts to the same

[23] *Humanae Vitae*, 21.

measures as are regarded as lawful by married people in the solution of a particular family difficulty? Who will prevent public authorities from favoring those contraceptive methods which they consider more effective? Should they regard this as necessary, they may even impose their use on everyone. It could well happen, therefore, that when people, either individually or in family or social life, experience the inherent difficulties of the divine law and are determined to avoid them, they may give into the hands of public authorities the power to intervene in the most personal and intimate responsibility of husband and wife.[24]

I don't think even Pope Paul VI had any idea just how prophetic his encyclical was. Morality has sunk to an all-time low. You probably couldn't find too many people who would disagree with that claim. If you want to check out that theory quickly for yourself, turn on the TV. Watch some of the reruns of the shows popular when I was growing up, such as *Bewitched* or *The Brady Bunch*. Then switch to any one of the despicable programs that Americans now deem not only acceptable but a revered form of entertainment, such as *Family Guy*, *How I Met Your Mother*, or that all too familiar show we've already referenced more than once, thanks to all of its not-so-redeeming qualities, *Desperate Housewives*.

As to the Pope's second point, that respect for women would dramatically decrease, isn't it quite obvious that women are more objectified in our culture than ever before? Since the beginning of *Playboy* magazine, pornography has gone more and more mainstream. With the Internet, porn has spread like a wildfire with more children accessing it than ever thought imaginable. With sexual content in all forms of media increasing and becoming more blatant by the day, the word *pornography* is fast losing its meaning. Even programming aimed at

[24] Ibid., 17.

young children—on the Disney Channel, for example—is focused on romantic relationships. Stars like Britney Spears and Miley Cyrus, whose careers as entertainers were launched by Disney, have encouraged girls to dress and act provocatively. Cashing in on the trend are the purveyors of immodest clothing for girls ages seven and up.

Regarding the third point, about governments requiring the use of contraceptives in order to limit their populations, take a look at China. In that country, couples are permitted only one child. If after having one child a woman is found to be pregnant, she can be forced to undergo an abortion. In October 2010, a Chinese woman who was eight months pregnant was dragged from her home and forced to have an abortion.[25] The story received worldwide attention after it was discovered that a dozen government officials had entered the woman's home and dragged her, kicking and screaming, to the hospital, where doctors injected her with a drug to kill her unborn child. It sounds like a scene from a horror film, but this is not Hollywood—this is real life in the twenty-first century, thanks to the onslaught of contraception. It would take another book—several books, actually—to detail the sterilization campaigns that are under way around the globe. The Population Research Institute estimates that such campaigns have been used in at least twenty-four countries and that they have, "to a greater or lesser extent, used coercion to reach sterilization targets, even though the practice of targets or setting goals has been condemned by international agreement".[26]

---

[25] Peter Simpson, "China Forces Women into Abortion at EIGHT Months for Breaching One-Child Policy", London Daily Mail Online, October 22, 2010, http://dailymail.co.uk/news/article-1322601/China-forces-woman-abortion-EIGHT-months-breaching-child-policy.html.

[26] "Fact Sheet on Sterilization Campaigns around the World", Congressional Briefing, February 23, 1998, Population Research Institute, http://

As to Pope Paul VI's final prediction regarding contraception, that we would lose reverence for the whole human person, the Church was right again. Just look at some of the practices, considered by many to be medical advances, that use human beings as if they were factories or the products of manufacturing—egg harvesting, cloning attempts, in vitro fertilization, embryonic stem cell research, and surrogate motherhood.

Tale of Two Anniversaries

In 2008 the Catholic Church marked the fortieth anniversary of *Humanae Vitae*. Many Catholic organizations, dioceses, Vatican councils, and individual parishes did their best to raise awareness on the importance and timeliness of the document, given all that has transpired since it was issued in 1968. That anniversary didn't receive nearly the public attention garnered by the fiftieth anniversary of the birth control pill on May 9, 2010. (Frankly, I thought it was downright diabolical that the pill's anniversary fell on Mother's Day; the anniversary, of course, came with a big media frenzy that made it appear as if the pill were the savior of womankind when just the opposite is true.)

With all the hoopla celebrating the pill, there was no mention of whether it delivered on its promises. When the pill was introduced, it was promoted as the solution to many social problems. It was expected to, among other things, (1) address population control issues, (2) improve marriages, and (3) result in fewer unwanted pregnancies.

Let's fast-forward fifty-plus years after the introduction of the pill—and see whether these promises have been

www.pop.org/content/fact-sheet-on-sterilization-campaigns-around-the-world-872.

fulfilled.[27] First, it is becoming clearer by the day that we need not control the population (that is, decrease population growth) but in fact to reverse dangerous trends related to *low* population levels around the world. We are not meeting replacement-rate fertility levels in many countries, especially on the European continent.

Since the pill, divorce has increased, not decreased, in America, and many couples are not even getting married at all: the number of cohabitating couples has greatly increased in recent years, according to a U.S. Census Bureau report. Between 2009 and 2010 there was a 13 percent increase in the number of opposite-sex couples living together.[28] Meanwhile, the institution of marriage, as between one man and one woman, is regularly challenged in the courts, the direct result of separating sex from procreation.

Finally, regarding out-of-wedlock pregnancy rates, 41 percent of all children in America are born out of wedlock; that number rises to 71 percent when we look at the African American community.[29]

> In the early 1960s the out-of-wedlock pregnancy rate was about 6 percent; it is now 41 percent. And, of course, we must add the number of abortions each year that are the result of unwanted pregnancies. What is liberating about these realities? The children born to unwed mothers and the mothers themselves and all of the culture suffer greatly. It is astonishing that some people think the current rate of

[27] Population Research Institute, "The World's Vanishing Children", http://www.pop.org/content/the-worlds-vanishing-children-85.

[28] Rose M. Kreider, "Increase in Opposite-Sex Cohabitating Couples from 2009 to 2010", (working paper, Housing and Household Economic Statistics Division, U.S. Census Bureau, September 15, 2010), p. 1.

[29] National Center for Health Statistics, Centers for Disease Control and Prevention, "Changing Patterns of Nonmarital Childbearing in the United States", May 13, 2009, http://www.cdc.gov/nchs/data/databriefs/db18.htm.

unwed pregnancies can be reduced by providing more and better contraceptives. Why can't the policy makers see that our entertainment world glorifies sex outside of marriage? Why don't they use their influence to raise awareness of the damage done to everyone because of sex outside of marriage, facilitated by contraception and an irresponsible entertainment world?[30]

Adverse Health Effects of Contraception

The media blitz celebrating the birth control pill also failed to mention its adverse health effects. But as Janet Smith has pointed out, the media is not alone in its denial:

> The disturbing amount of duplicity and falsehood surrounding contraception continues to this day. Neither pharmaceutical companies nor physicians have been honest about the medical dangers of chemical contraceptives. The pill launched a whole set of chemical contraceptives, including Depo Provera, Ortho Evra, also known as the Patch, and Norplant. More and more studies . . . are linking contraception with increased incidences of some forms of cancer.[31]

In 2005 the World Health Organization classified the birth control pill as a group 1 carcinogen. The pill contains powerful steroids of estrogen and progesterone along with their synthetic equivalents. According to the Breast Cancer Prevention Institute, these steroids can "cause the breast tissue to grow which can result in mutations and ultimately cancers.

[30] Janet E. Smith, "Why Are the Media So Fixated on Condoms?" December 1, 2010, http://www.zenit.org/article-31127?1=english.
[31] Janet E. Smith, "In Focus: Uncovering a String of Lies", *Our Sunday Visitor*, May 2, 2010, http://www.osv.com/tabid/7621/itemid/6286/In-Focus-Uncovering-a-string-of-lies.aspx.

Estrogens can act as direct carcinogens causing cancer cells to form." [32]

Just read the inserts in any set of birth control pills, and you will see that the pill can also cause high blood pressure, heart disease, and blood clots.

And regarding emotional health, although women who take the pill for birth control reasons are hoping it will help their sex lives, research shows that the pill actually lowers a woman's sex drive and can also cause weight gain and depression. Well, doesn't that make you want to run to your gynecologist and get a prescription!

Contraception and the Rise in Sexually Transmitted Diseases

Sexual promiscuity through unlimited access to contraception is sold to women as freedom; however, women usually end up paying a higher price for casual sex than do men. We know that the pill may prevent pregnancy, but it does not protect against the transmission of sexually transmitted diseases (STDs). According to the Centers for Disease Control and Prevention (CDC), STDs are at epidemic proportions in the United States and are considered a major public health threat. Nineteen million new cases of STDs are diagnosed each year, at a cost of $16.4 billion annually to the U.S. health care system. [33]

---

[32] *If It Is Not OK for Him to Take Steroids, Why Is It OK for Her?* (Poughkeepsie, N.Y.: Breast Cancer Prevention Institute, 2006), p. 2. Brochure available online at http://www.bcpinstitute.org/Steroid_brochure_why_let_her.pdf.

[33] Centers for Disease Control and Prevention, "2008 National STD Prevention Conference Draws Nation's Public Health Leaders Together to Confront Sexually Transmitted Diseases", March 10, 2008, http://www.cdc.gov/stdconference/2008/press/lead-release.htm.

The CDC also states that there is a much bigger cost to individuals in terms of long-term health consequences. For women, some STDs can lead to pelvic inflammatory disease, which can cause infertility. Genital human papillomavirus, or HPV, is thought to be one of the main causes of cervical cancer and can also lead to other types of cancer in the female reproductive system.

Let's take a look at a few alarming statistics:

- In 2009 some 1,244,180 cases of chlamydia were reported to the CDC, the largest number of cases reported to the CDC for any condition.
- In 2009 the overall rate at which women became infected with chlamydia was almost three times the rate for men.
- Since 2006, chlamydia infections have increased 19 percent.[34]

In late 2010, concerns over STDs in Britain were so high that researchers felt compelled to start working on a way to use cell phones to perform pathology tests. According to the British newspaper the *Guardian*, plenty of money was already invested in the idea by the time the first stories on the possible new app went viral around the world.

> Mobile phones and computers will soon be able to diagnose sexually transmitted diseases under innovative plans to cut the UK's rising rate of herpes, chlamydia and gonorrhoea among young people.
>
> Doctors and technology experts are developing small devices, similar to pregnancy testing kits, that will tell someone quickly and privately if he has caught an infection through sexual contact.

[34] "Chlamydia–CDC Fact Sheet", http://www.cdc.gov/std/chlamydia/STDFact-Chlamydia.htm.

People who suspect they have been infected will be able to put urine or saliva on to a computer chip about the size of a USB chip, plug it into their phone or computer and receive a diagnosis within minutes, telling them which, if any, sexually transmitted infection (STI) they have.[35]

Sending the Wrong Message

One of the saddest aspects of the selling of sex is how the assumption that casual sex is okay is being passed on to the next generation of women. This message is now being hidden behind the veneer of protective medicine. I am talking in particular here about a vaccine designed to protect against some types of cervical cancer. This vaccine, called Gardasil, is being pushed by pediatricians and others in the medical profession as a way to protect sexually active girls from HPV, which, as we noted above, is an STD that can cause cervical cancer. There are two issues to look at here: the issue of the problems with the drug itself and the overall signal it is sending to girls about sex outside of marriage.

Complaints have been piling up about the safety of the product. According to numerous published reports, as of late 2008—a mere two years after Gardasil's release—the CDC had received nearly ten thousand complaints concerning the vaccine. Complaints included headaches, fainting spells, blood clots, paralysis, and even death.[36] Papers from the FDA itself detailing adverse reactions to Gardasil—including sixteen new deaths—were released September 29,

[35] Denis Campbell, "Mobile Phone Kits to Diagnose STDs", *Guardian*, November 5, 2010, http://www.guardian.co.uk/uk/2010/nov/05/new-test-mobile-phones-diagnose-stds.

[36] "Potential Problems with Gardasil Reported: Is Cervical Cancer Vaccine Safe?" TheBostonChannel.com, September 25, 2008, http://www.thebostonchannel.com/r/17557347/detail.html.

2010, by Judicial Watch, a public interest group that investigates government corruption.[37]

Merck (the drug company behind the vaccine) and the government still stand behind the product, claiming that Gardasil is an effective protection against HPV, which is a very common STD, especially among women.

So we have established the possibility of some severe and very adverse side effects that may occur with Gardasil. But more important, when a tween or teen girl is given the vaccine, what are we saying to her? We are saying the same thing when we give her birth control pills or condoms: "You're probably going to have sex soon anyway, so better safe than sorry."

We have bought into this idea of "safe sex" when it is the biggest oxymoron going. There is no such thing as "safe sex" outside of marriage. With or without contraception and vaccines, young people engaging in premarital sex are risking their health and harming their souls. Sexually active teens have a higher rate of substance abuse and depression compared to those who abstain from sexual activity. Surely, the using and being used, the broken promises and broken hearts take their toll.[38] Why don't we love or trust young people enough to promote abstaining from sexual relations until marriage? Why aren't we telling them they are daughters of the King of Kings? They

[37] "Judicial Watch Uncovers FDA Records Detailing 16 New Deaths Tied to Gardasil", September 28, 2010, http://www.judicialwatch.org/news/2010/sep/judicial-watch-uncovers-fda-records-detailing-16-new-deaths-tied-gardasil.

[38] "Teens: Sex, Drugs, and Depression?", CBS News, February 11, 2009, http://www.cbsnews.com/stories/2005/09/20/health/webmd/main870398.shtml; Public Institute for Research and Evaluation, "Adolescent Depression and Suicide Risk: Association with Sex and Drug Behavior", October 2004, http://www.ncbi.nlm.nih.gov/pubmed/15450635.

need to know they deserve better than the "safe sex" way of life, which is not safe at all.

Think about the young woman you met in the beginning of this chapter. She was convinced that she had to be sexually active because no one had told her otherwise. How sad. Research shows abstinence education works—and works well. A study released in 2010[39] showed that abstinence education is "highly effective in reducing sexual activity among youth".[40] The study also showed that "safe sex" programs (promoting only contraceptive use) and "comprehensive" sex education programs (teaching both abstinence and contraceptive use) were ineffective. The study was published in the *Archives of Pediatrics and Adolescent Medicine*, which is published by the American Medical Association. "The study found that the probability of ever having sexual intercourse [by the 24-month follow-up] was approximately 15 percentage points lower among teens in the abstinence-only program than those in condom-promoting courses or those undergoing no sex education."[41]

Conclusion

It has been said that the definition of insanity is doing the same thing over and over again and expecting different results. We (and I use that pronoun *we* to describe our world today)

[39]John B. Jemmott III, Loretta S. Jemmott, and Geoffrey T. Fong, "Efficacy of a Theory-Based Abstinence-Only Intervention over 24 Months: A Randomized Controlled Trial with Young Adolescents", *Archives of Pediatrics and Adolescent Medicine* 164 (February 2010): 152–59.

[40] "Studies and Statistics: New Study: Abstinence Education Effective; Comprehensive Sex Ed a Big Flop", Abstinence Clearinghouse, February 3, 2010, http://www.abstinence.net/library/index.php?entryid=4590.

[41]Kathleen Gilbert, "Abstinence-Only Education Linked to Decreased Promiscuity in High-Risk Teens: Study", LifeSiteNews.com, February 1, 2010, http://www.lifesitenews.com/news/archive/ldn/2010/feb/10020108.

are determined to do what we want to do as often as we want to do it and with whomever we want to do it, and we're also telling our young people to do the same. We want to have our way even when the stakes are high. I've given you, the reader, only a thumbnail sketch of the research showing the ugly reality of taking sexuality outside of God's plan. I don't think I am exaggerating when I say that the sexual revolution has been disastrous.

The world tells us that the Church is archaic and out of touch, even backward, with her teachings. But wait just a minute here—the Church does not teach that sex is wrong. Who created sex in the first place? It wasn't Johnson & Johnson. It was Father, Son, and Holy Spirit. Marriage, the union of a man and a woman, is the closest representation on earth of the relationship between the Holy Trinity and also of the relationship between Christ and His Church. Jesus is the bridegroom, and the Church is His bride. (I hope you consult the list of helpful organizations and web-sites contained in my resource list, located on pp. 156–58 of this book.)

Statistics support the Church's teaching that marriage is the proper context for sex. Research shows that about 40 percent of married women said that their sex life was emotionally and physically satisfying, compared to about 30 percent of single women. Research also shows that cohabitating couples do not have the same type of commitment as married couples and are less likely to be sexually faithful.[42]

Let's do a quick review. Accepting the messages of the culture leads many into sexual relationships outside of marriage. These relationships can lead to serious sin, serious

[42] Richard Niolon, review of *The Case for Marriage: Why Married People Are Happier, Healthier, and Better Off Financially*, by Linda J. Waite and Maggie Gallagher (New York: Doubleday, 2000), PsychPage, http://www.psychpage.com/family/library/brwaitgalligher.html.

physical and emotional illness, and serious problems for society. The fruits of these relationships are higher divorce rates, more abortions, more children born out of wedlock, increased numbers of STDs, major health complications, higher infertility rates, and increased objectification of women. Listening to God and keeping sex right where it is supposed to be—between one man and one woman, husband and wife in the marital bed—helps us avoid all of these troubles, and more. So which is more conducive to human happiness, "free sex" or the teaching of the Church?

Let me close with some additional words of wisdom from Janet Smith and also some words from *the* Word, as in God, Himself.

> Rather than "celebrating" the 50th anniversary [of the birth control pill], our culture should take an honest look at what the pill (and its cousins) have done to our culture. It may come to see that the Church, rather than being retrograde and an obstacle to progress, is one of the few voices of sanity in a culture gone mad.[43]

For I know the plans I have for you, says the LORD, plans for welfare and not for evil, to give you a future and a hope.

—Jeremiah 29:11

---

[43] Smith, "In Focus: Uncovering a String of Lies".

Questions for Reflection

1. How has the culture affected your beliefs and practices regarding sexuality?

2. Are you following Church teaching regarding contraception?

3. Have you read the Church teachings on contraception? (See, for example, *Humanae Vitae*, *Evangelium Vitae*, and the *Catechism of the Catholic Church* [nos. 2370 and 2399].)

4. Did you consult a priest or seek some sort of spiritual direction regarding the issue of contraception?

5. If you did consult a priest, what sort of advice or guidance did you receive, and was that advice in support of Church teaching?

6. If you have not been following Church teaching, what immediate steps can you take to change your practices?

7. Are you willing to take a closer look at any media habits that you may have that may be hindering your spiritual life and relationship with God, especially in the area of sexuality and contraception usage?

Chapter 5

Mirror, Mirror:

Discovering Our True Beauty
Inside and Out

Beauty without virtue is a flower without perfume.

—French proverb

One of the most moving letters or e-mails I ever received after giving a talk came from a high school senior. It was a few weeks after I gave my "Choices and Challenges Facing Today's Teens" presentation at a Midwestern high school. In this particular presentation I discuss my own struggles with peer pressure, media influence, and an eating disorder and try to show teens how the bad choices and good choices I made when I was their age are still playing out in my life decades later. My comments must have had an impact because Mary (not her real name) wrote the following letter and then asked her high school principal to send it to me.

> Hello:
>
> I have been at this high school for three and a half years, and this is the first time I remember someone coming in to talk about self-image. I really want to thank

you for the talk you gave! It really touched me deeply. The first friend I made in high school was bulimic, and I came close to it too. I then began cutting myself and continued with that for several months. My parents got help for me, and at the end of my junior year I finally came out of depression. I was able to return to God, and I've never felt happier. I'll never allow myself to lose Him again or fall back into that depressing state of mind. Hearing your talk today really helped solidify this in my heart. I am so grateful for your talk and your testimony.

A close friend of mine is now suffering from anorexia. I was the only person she confided in, and I finally had enough sense to tell the school guidance counselor about it. Now, all I can do is pray she's getting the help she needs.

Thank you so much for taking the time to talk to our school. A lot of people needed to hear what you had to say. Even though my three-year depression has fortunately ended, I felt I got a lot from your story.

God bless,
Mary

For a teen to take the time to sit down and compose a handwritten personal note in today's instantaneous world of texts and e-mails, and then take it to the principal to make sure it gets delivered, says an awful lot about how important she thought it was to let me know that I was hitting a major nerve. Even in her particular place of learning, which happened to be an outstanding, orthodox Catholic high school with strong parental involvement, Eucharistic adoration, weekly Mass, and a solid theology department, the problems of the world still crept in.

What also struck me were her struggles and challenges. She was a high school senior, and most of her high school years had been extremely painful. What was so horrible in this young woman's life that it caused her to have so many issues at such a tender age?

We women certainly can't blame the media entirely for our problems with self-image, but as Mary's story strongly implies, we can't ignore the role played by the media either. We can surmise a number of things about Mary's life from her note, including the fact that she came from a loving family. Her parents did not ignore her problems and sought professional and spiritual help. She goes to a good Catholic school with a faith-filled environment. But even with solid resources, she obviously struggled with peer pressure and self-esteem issues. Some of the influence—in fact, I would venture to say a great deal of the influence—is likely media based. I know this not only from my research and expertise in media influence but also from my own struggle with anorexia nervosa.

My Experiences with an Eating Disorder

There are a variety of reasons and causes for eating disorders, and media influence is definitely part of the mix. In my case, I knew at a very young age that I was going to pursue a career in broadcasting. I realized that appearance would definitely matter if I planned to be on television. I have always struggled with my weight; I was often teased by my classmates for my abundance of "baby fat" and was determined to get in shape. When I was about twelve years old, I explained my hurt and concern over my weight issues to my mother, and she decided to consult our family pediatrician. The doctor agreed that a reasonable weight loss of ten to fifteen pounds was fine as long as I ate a healthy diet. We followed the doctor's instruction, and I lost weight. I felt better but wasn't satisfied.

My weight issues turned into a bout with an eating disorder in the early seventies, at a time when such illnesses were just being discovered and diagnosed—and at a time when superthin TV and movie stars were taking center stage. Supermodel Twiggy burst onto the scene in the 1960s, and in the seventies one of the most popular cover girls, Susan Dey, became an overnight TV sensation after landing a major role on the popular ABC situation comedy *The Partridge Family*. Everyone wanted to look like her and be her. After all, she was tall and thin and wore really cute clothes. But more important, every day she had the incredible opportunity to work side by side with every teen girl's crush back then, David Cassidy. Who could ask for anything more? It wasn't until much later that Dey revealed that she had dealt with anorexia nervosa and bulimia while starring on the popular hit show. The actress' weight dropped to ninety-two pounds, and she reportedly stopped menstruating. My weight dropped to eighty-nine pounds. I stopped menstruating, and I ended up in a local hospital. I just wanted to be skinny; I badly wanted to look like my role model. Little did I know that my role model was suffering from eating disorders.

Since there was not much help available for eating disorders back then, the doctors merely told me that unless I gained some weight they could not allow me to go home and that my continued hospitalization could possibly affect high school enrollment. Their warnings weren't enough to get me eating again. It wasn't enough, either, to make the weight struggles and issues go away for good. I am not a doctor or a psychologist, but I can honestly say that nearly thirty years later, the eating disorder in some small way is still with me. (In a 1993 newspaper interview, Dey concurred, saying that twenty years after her own eating disorder experience, her life was still plagued by anorexia and bulimia.)[1] I eat right, exercise, and maintain a size 8. But there is still that voice in the back of my head that gnaws at me and tells me that I should be a size 6 or smaller. And my weight can still fluctuate up and down if I am not careful.

My challenges, and Susan Dey's challenges, began back in the seventies. We didn't have MTV. We didn't have Facebook or other social media. We didn't have a TV and a computer in every bedroom. There certainly wasn't as much sexual content in media programming as there is today, and we didn't have as much media being thrown at us 24-7 and making us constantly aware of our appearance. Even so, I suffered from an eating disorder and self-esteem issues; I can only imagine what today's girls and women of all ages are facing with the pressure to be superthin, stylish, and on top of it, a sex goddess, is coming at them from all directions.

> Sadly, even though there is a much greater awareness of eating disorders, along with efforts to address the illnesses through different types of treatment programs, eating disorders are still on the rise—and the problems are affecting younger and younger children. In December 2010 the American Academy of Pediatrics released a report showing that eating disorders skyrocketed between 1999 and 2006 among young people, including those twelve and younger.[2]

Between 1999 and 2006, there was a 119 percent jump in hospitalizations resulting from eating disorders in children under age twelve. There also has been a rise in severe cases of both anorexia and bulimia. The American Academy of Pediatrics recommends that all adolescents and

---

[1] "Celebrities with Eating Disorders", http://www.caringonline.com/eatdis/celebrities_s.html.

[2] David Rosen, for the AAP Committee on Adolescence, "Identification and Management of Eating Disorders in Children and Adolescents", *Pediatrics* 126 (December 2010): 1240–53.

pre-teens be screened for eating disorders at their regular check-ups to address these issues.[3]

The Human Body: Sharing in the Dignity of the Image of God

Somehow we have to get back to basics and find a balance. Our faith doesn't tell us that we can't look and feel our best—but there has to be moderation. Our image, our understanding, must come from our Creator, as explained so beautifully in paragraph 364 of the *Catechism*: "The human body shares in the dignity of 'the image of God': it is a human body precisely because it is animated by a spiritual soul, and it is the whole person that is intended to become, in the body of Christ, a temple of the Spirit." In other words, a person is not just a physical body. Nor is he just a spiritual being floating around the earth.

The *Catechism* goes on to quote *Gaudium et Spes*, a document from the Second Vatican Council:

> Man, though made of body and soul, is a unity. Through his very bodily condition he sums up in himself the elements of the material world. Through him they are thus brought to their highest perfection and can raise their voice in praise freely given to the Creator. For this reason man may not despise his bodily life. Rather he is obliged to regard his body as good and to hold it in honor since God has created it and will raise it up on the last day.[4]

[3] Susan Brady, "Rise in Teenage Eating Disorders", November 29, 2010, HealthNews, http://www.healthnews.com/en/Categories/Family-Health/Rise-in-Teenage-Eating-Disorders.

[4] *Gaudium et Spes* (December 7, 1965), 14; quoted in the *Catechism of the Catholic Church*, no. 364.

I think the word *despise* here is key. Not too many of us love our bodies. As someone who speaks to teens and women regularly, I can pretty much say that most females don't like what they see when they look in the mirror. Many, actually, do despise their appearance and would never consider describing themselves as beautiful.

Women and Self-Esteem: The Research

One of the most interesting and well-known studies to back up my claim that females have little self-esteem comes from a worldwide effort called the Campaign for Real Beauty, initiated by the Dove soap company in 2004. *The Real Truth about Beauty: A Global Report* was commissioned to "further the global understanding of women, beauty and well-being—and the relationship between them".[5] Concern over the culture's portrayal of beauty and the unattainable images constantly paraded before women was the impetus for the study. Researchers interviewed some thirty-two hundred women aged eighteen to sixty-four in ten countries: the United States, Great Britain, Canada, France, Italy, Portugal, Brazil, the Netherlands, Japan, and Argentina. Not surprisingly, women around the world share similar feelings. They don't have much confidence in their appearance, and that lack of confidence is being aided and abetted by media messages.

- 68 percent of those questioned strongly agreed that "the media and advertising set an unrealistic standard of beauty that most women can never achieve."
- Only 2 percent of the women surveyed felt comfortable describing themselves as beautiful.

[5] *The Real Truth about Beauty: A Global Report*, September 2004, Campaign for Real Beauty Worldwide, http://www.campaignforrealbeauty.com/uploadedfiles/dove_white_paper_final.pdf.

- Women felt this way regardless of their age.
- Almost three-quarters, or 72 percent, saw themselves as average.
- 63 percent of those questioned said women are expected to be more physically attractive than their mothers.
- 60 percent said society expects women to enhance their physical attractiveness.
- 46 percent strongly agreed with the statement "Only the most physically attractive women are portrayed in popular culture."

Apparently women are so convinced that their worth depends upon their outward appearance that quite a few women who work outside the home think that cosmetic surgery could be connected to success on the job. I wonder what Gloria Steinem would say if she saw the results of a 2009 telephone survey of 115 million working-age women conducted by the American Society of Plastic Surgeons. "Faced with news of increasing layoffs, straining economic times, and a belief that hiring is based on looks, millions of American women are looking at cosmetic medical procedures to give them a competitive edge in the workplace."[6]

- 13 percent of those surveyed said they would consider having a cosmetic medical procedure specifically to make them more confident and more competitive in the job market.
- 3 percent said they've already had cosmetic surgery to increase their perceived value in the workplace.

[6] American Society of Plastic Surgeons, "Women in the Workforce Link Cosmetic Surgery to Success", news release, February 10, 2009, http://www.plasticsurgery.org/Media/Press_Releases/Women_in_the_Workforce_Link_Cosmetic_Surgery_to_Success.html.

- 73 percent (or 84 million) believed appearance and youthful looks play a part in getting hired, getting a promotion, or getting new clients.
- 80 percent say having cosmetic medical procedures can boost a person's confidence.[7]

Silly me. I thought that working hard or maybe going back to school for more education or training would be valued by today's modern women. Who knew career advancement was all about a smaller nose and a bigger cup size?

The Sexualization of Girls

The two aforementioned studies surveyed women in their late teens and older. But the younger generation doesn't fare much better when it comes to their opinions of themselves. An American Psychological Association (APA) report grabbed major headlines in 2007 with its honest look at how young girls are being objectified by the mass media. In its *Sexualization of Girls* study, the APA gave detailed and chilling documentation concerning the impact of media content, claiming that concern over the issue is widespread. "Journalists, child advocacy organizations, parents, and psychologists have argued that the sexualization of girls is a broad and increasing problem and is harmful to girls. The APA Task Force on the Sexualization of Girls was formed in response to these expressions of public concern." [8]

As we have seen, the encyclical *Humanae Vitae* warned that an oversexualized culture that accepted contraception and abortion would be harmful, not helpful, to women.

[7] Ibid.
[8] *Report of the APA Task Force on the Sexualization of Girls: Executive Summary* (Washington, D.C.: American Psychological Association, 2007), p. 1, http://www.apa.org/pi/women/programs/girls/report-summary.pdf.

Well, the APA has documented the harm done to girls when their sexuality is overemphasized:

> Research links sexualization with three of the most common mental health problems of girls and women: eating disorders, low self-esteem and depression or depressed mood.... Research also links exposure to sexualized female ideals with lower self-esteem, negative mood, and depressive symptoms among adolescent girls and women. In addition to mental health consequences of sexualization, research suggests that girls' and women's physical health may also be negatively affected, albeit indirectly....
>
> Frequent exposure to media images that sexualize girls and women affects how girls conceptualize femininity and sexuality. Girls and young women who more frequently consume or engage with mainstream media content offer stronger endorsement of sexual stereotypes that depict women as sexual objects.[9]

The APA took a long, hard look at published research on media content. They looked at just about every form of media, including the Internet, TV, music videos and lyrics, movies, video games, and advertising. According to an APA press release on the report, sexualization was defined as occurring "when a person's value comes only from her/his sexual appeal or behavior, to the exclusion of other characteristics, and when a person is sexually objectified, e.g., made into a *thing* for another's sexual use".[10]

Notice the terminology in that last line? Let's compare it to section 17 of *Humanae Vitae*: "Another effect that gives cause

[9] Ibid., p. 3.

[10] American Psychological Association, "Sexualization of Girls Is Linked to Common Mental Health Problems in Girls and Women—Eating Disorders, Low Self-Esteem, and Depression; An APA Task Force Reports", news release, February 19, 2007, http://www.apa.org/news/press/releases/2007/02/sexualization.aspx. Emphasis in original.

for alarm is that a man who grows accustomed to the use of contraceptive methods may forget the reverence due to a woman, and, disregarding her physical and emotional equilibrium, reduce her to being a mere instrument for the satisfaction of his own desires, no longer considering her as his partner whom he should surround with care and affection." [11]

Pope Paul VI was referring here to what could happen—and has happened—in marriage when contraception enters the picture. The APA, a very procontraception and pro–"safe sex" organization, is not blaming contraception for the objectification of girls; it is blaming an oversexualized culture: "Massive exposure to media among youth creates the potential for massive exposure to portrayals that sexualize women and girls and teach girls that women are sexual objects." The APA study named a number of musicians that sexualize women and girls: Madonna, Kid Rock, Britney Spears, and Christina Aguilera. Lady Gaga was not yet on the scene, otherwise she surely would have made the list. In the magazine category, *YM, Teen, Mademoiselle,* [12] *Seventeen,* and *Glamour* were mentioned as "encouraging young women to think of themselves as sexual objects whose lives were not complete unless sexually connected with a man". [13]

The Church maintains that the root of oversexualization lies in mankind going against God's plan for sexuality and making contraception and abortion the norm. In *Humanae Vitae,* the Pope predicted that it would be only a matter of time before we would see the cultural shift we are now experiencing if contraception became widely accepted. You

[11] Paul VI, *Humanae Vitae* (July 25, 1968), 17, Holy See website, http://www.vatican.va/holy_father/paul_vi/encyclicals/documents/hf_p-vi_enc_25071968_humanae-vitae_en.html.

[12] *YM, Teen,* and *Mademoiselle* are no longer published.

[13] American Psychological Association, *Report on the Sexualization of Girls* (full report), p. 8.

don't have to be Catholic, or even Christian, to make the obvious contraception connection; even if the APA itself doesn't make that leap, its report surely provides data to support this conclusion.

Many other studies and numerous stories in the secular press highlight the obsession women and girls have with their appearance and the need to look and act pretty and sexy at a younger and younger age. In March 2009 *Newsweek* did an excellent report investigating the influence of media on girls, specifically zeroing in on our culture's obsession with beauty. In "Generation Diva: How Our Obsession with Beauty Is Changing Our Kids", the reporter used the reality series *Toddlers and Tiaras*, aired on cable network's TLC, as one example of the obsession with appearance and the sexualization of girls. The article mentioned two-year-old Marleigh, who was filmed getting a makeup treatment in preparation for an upcoming pageant. It described a scene in which the toddler was sitting in front of the mirror "smothering her face with blush and lipstick".

> Reared on reality TV and celebrity makeovers, girls as young as Marleigh are using beauty products earlier, spending more and still feeling worse about themselves. Four years ago, a study by the NPD Group showed that, on average, women began using beauty products at 17. Today, the average is 13—and that's got to be an overstatement. According to market-research firm Experian, 43 percent of 6- to 9-year-olds are already using lipstick or lip gloss; 38 percent use hairstyling products; and 12 percent use other cosmetics. And the level of interest is making the girls of "Toddlers & Tiaras" look ordinary." [14]

[14] Jessica Bennett, "Generation Diva: How Our Obsession with Beauty Is Changing Our Kids", *Newsweek*, March 30, 2009, http://www. newsweek.com/2009/03/29/generation-diva.html.

For the APA, it's the "sexualization" of girls; for *Newsweek*, it's the "diva-ization" of girls, which occurs before they hit the tween years. No matter what they call it, social observers see the same thing: pop culture is influencing our girls to focus more and more on being sexually attractive to men. Is that so surprising when we consider what a variety of other researchers have found?

- Virtually every media form provides ample evidence of the sexualization of women and girls including TV, music videos, music lyrics, movies, magazines, sports media, video games, the Internet, and advertising.[15]
- 27 percent of girls surveyed by *Teen People Magazine* say they hardly ever feel confident about their bodies.[16]
- Advertisers spend more than $12 billion per year to reach the youth market.[17]

The problem of media influence on women and girls was such a concern for Nicole Clark that the former Elite International model exposed the problem in the 2009 documentary film *Cover Girl Culture: Awakening the Media Generation*. The film, which is an in-depth look at the fashion and advertising world, challenges the media to send young people a better message: "Being thin, pretty and sexy and having lots of 'stuff' is not what brings happiness. Yet this is the fervent message young girls receive hundreds of times every day. It's time to step up and be responsible about what is important in life and have integrity in the media/

---

[15] "Sexualization of Girls", American Psychological Association (February 2007), http://www.apa.org/pi/women/programs/girls/report.aspx.

[16] "*Teen People* Releases Results of First Body Image Survey" (August 2005), PR Newswire Press Release, July 5, 2005.

[17] *Report of the APA Task Force on Advertising and Children*, http://apa.org/pubs/info/reports/advertising-children.aspx.

advertising world. The media has jumped on the band-wagon with 'Eco-friendly' campaigns so now it's time to promote 'Truth to Youth' or 'Kindness to Kids.' " [18]

True Beauty

The message women and girls need to hear is that true beauty is not a physical reality. After we learn that a phys-ically attractive woman has acted badly, aren't we disap-pointed? Don't we even think less of her appearance than we did before? How many of us think Paris Hilton or Lind-sey Lohan is pretty? How many of us think homely and wrinkled Mother Teresa was radiant? The reason for these reactions is that true beauty is a spiritual reality; it comes from the soul. When we act selfishly we are not attractive. When we behave with goodness and kindness, the beauty of our souls shines through.

Every well-dressed woman understands that the clothes she wears should attract attention to her face, and particu-larly to her eyes, not to her body parts. Why? Because the eyes are the windows into the soul. Dressing well, then, requires modesty. The *Catechism of the Catholic Church*, in paragraphs 2520–27, defines purity and helps us understand the importance of modesty. Here we can see the connec-tion between purity, modesty, and protecting the dignity of the person created in the image and likeness of God. "The forms taken by modesty vary from one culture to another. Everywhere, however, modesty exists as an intuition of the spiritual dignity proper to man. It is born with the awak-ening consciousness of being a subject. Teaching modesty

---

[18] "Bio", *Cover Girl Culture: Awakening the Media Generation* official web site, accessed March 3, 2011, http://www.covergirlculture.com/?page_id=13.

to children and adolescents means awakening in them respect for the human person." [19]

It took years of pain, struggle, and study for me to figure out that I was more than my body. I had to learn the hard way—through an eating disorder and other challenges—that what matters most is what is on the inside, not the outside, and that God's plan, not my plan or the world's plan, is what's best for me.

That said, the Catholic Church does not teach that women have to walk around wearing sacks and no makeup. After all, as Catholic author, speaker, and EWTN radio and TV host Johnette Benkovic says, "Wearing makeup is an act of charity." Indeed, it is!

Saint Peter wrote that a woman's beauty should not come from outward adornment but from a gentle spirit (cf. 1 Pet 3:3–4). As Scripture scholars explain, these verses were written during a time when some women spent most of their days fixing their hair and clothes. Peter wanted them to know that God sees and loves women for who they are, not what they look like. Jesus wants us to concentrate on the beauty of our souls by developing our virtues, not our eye shadow collection.

We are called to treat our bodies as temples of the Holy Spirit: "Do you not know that your body is a temple of the Holy Spirit within you, which you have from God? You are not your own; you were bought with a price. So glorify God in your body" (1 Cor 6:19–20). We can glorify God with our bodies by exercising the virtues of modesty and moderation. One of the many things I love about being Catholic is how balanced the Church is; she steers us away from extremes, in this case the extremes of vanity on one hand and self-neglect on the other. The body was created

[19] *Catechism of the Catholic Church*, no. 2524.

by God in His image and likeness. It is not a bad thing to be hidden or of which we need to be ashamed. Nor is it to be exposed indecently and treated as an object.

If only women could see themselves as Christ sees them, as daughters of the King, we would be more fulfilled and less prone to hours of agony in front of a mirror. Why did I take so many cues from the culture instead of from Christ and the Church? Why did I allow my young body to be ravaged by an eating disorder at such a crucial point in my life? Why do some women believe their professional stock will go up with plastic surgery versus additional experience, education, or training? Why are so many women of all ages dressing suggestively to attract attention to their bodies? Sadly, the answer to these questions is that women are trying to be loved by measuring up to an image of female beauty that has been thrust upon them by our sex-obsessed culture, an image that is impossible to imitate or maintain.

In his 1995 Letter to Women, John Paul II noted that it's time for us women to see ourselves, and for the world to see us, as God sees us: as dignified daughters whose contribution to society—as mothers, religious sisters, workers, artists, and members of the various professions—is invaluable. "To this great, immense feminine 'tradition' humanity owes a debt which can never be repaid. Yet how many women have been and continue to be valued more for their physical appearance than for their skill, their professionalism, their intellectual abilities, their deep sensitivity; in a word, the very dignity of their being!" [20]

Of course, society will not value women for their unique "feminine genius", as John Paul II called it, until they learn

---

[20] "Letter of Pope John Paul II to Women" (June 29, 1995), 3, Holy See website, http://www.vatican.va/holy_father/john_paul_ii/letters/documents/hf_jp-ii_let_29061995_women_en.html.

to value and respect themselves. And as we will see in the next chapter, the Catholic Church is the best place to do that.

Questions for Reflection

1. Have your media habits caused you to spend too much time and effort on your outward appearance?
2. Have your media habits caused you to experience lower self-esteem or a poor self-image?
3. What is your definition of beauty?
4. How was your definition of beauty formed?
5. Would you describe yourself as beautiful?
6. How much of your happiness or self-worth is based on your weight or appearance?
7. Have you ever felt objectified?
8. What types of changes would you like to see in the media or culture in terms of the way women are portrayed?

Chapter 6

Our Biggest Fan,
Our Greatest Liberator

Jesus, His Church, and the
Dignity of Women

The women *are the first at the tomb*. They are the first to
find it empty. They are the first to hear: "He is not here.
He has risen, as he said." They are the first to embrace his
feet. They are also the first to be called to announce this
truth to the Apostles.

—John Paul II, *Mulieris Dignitatem*
(emphasis in original)

It is important to view the Bible, along with the teachings
of the Catholic Church, as a big yes instead of a long list of
noes. Benedict XVI stressed this point early in his pontificate.
Although he was emphasizing the need to teach young people the beauty of God's commandments, his words of wisdom, I believe, need to be heard by everyone in the Church:

It is especially adolescents and young people, who feel within
them the pressing call to love, who need to be freed from
the widespread prejudice that Christianity, with its commandments and prohibitions, sets too many obstacles in the
path of the joy of love and, in particular, prevents people
from fully enjoying the happiness that men and women find

in their love for one another. On the contrary, Christian faith and ethics do not wish to stifle love but to make it healthy, strong and truly free: this is the exact meaning of the Ten Commandments, which are not a series of "noes" but a great "yes" to love and to life.[1]

For far too long, many Americans have looked upon the moral teaching of the Catholic Church as restrictive and oppressive. Most of the dissent, as has been already detailed, centers on the hot-button issues of abortion and contraception. But as the Holy Father pointed out, true joy and happiness are found in following God's plan, not in making up our own rules.

Because abortion and contraception are used to control childbearing, which, let's face it, burdens women far more than men, feminists say the Church's sexual morality is sexist. Feminists, ignoring the Church's blessing on Natural Family Planning, accuse the Catholic hierarchy of wanting to keep women "in their place" with one pregnancy after another.

Feminists also take aim at another area of Church teaching that relates to women: the all-male priesthood. By excluding women from the priesthood, they argue, the Church is excluding women from leadership positions. Why would the Church do that unless it thought women were inferior to men?

The Catholic Priesthood: Discriminatory toward Women?

On the surface, excluding women from the priesthood may seem unfair or unreasonable. But to get beyond the appearance, we have to be countercultural and do something the world has pretty much stopped doing: dig a little deeper.

---

[1] "Address to the Participants at the Ecclesial Convention of the Diocese of Rome" (Saint John Lateran Basilica, June 7, 2007), Holy See website, http://www.vatican.va/holy_father/benedict_xvi/speeches/2006/june/documents/hf_ben-xvi_spe_20060605_convegno-diocesano_en.html.

In examining how the Church treats women, let's go back to the beginning by taking a closer look at Scripture. In the Gospels, Jesus instituted the priesthood among His apostles at the Last Supper. Those who support women's ordination claim that Jesus limited the priesthood to men because He was restricted by the times in which He lived. In other words, the only reason that He didn't invite women to the Last Supper was because women's input was not valued two thousand years ago. Had Jesus physically walked the planet preaching and teaching in the twentieth or twenty-first centuries, feminists argue, He most certainly would have been more inclusive of women. The argument ignores, however, that Jesus was arrested by the Jewish priestly class for breaking their laws and customs. It overlooks that the way Jesus interacted with women astonished even his own disciples.

You're probably familiar with the Gospel story about Jesus and the Samaritan woman, also known as "the woman at the well". Saint John tells us that the apostles left Jesus sitting at a well when they went to the city to buy food. It was about noon, and a woman from Samaria then happened to come to draw water.

The timing is significant for the Samaritan woman. She was the local bad girl and knew that by going to the well at noon to fetch water there would less chance for her to be seen and insulted by townspeople, who would have wanted to avoid the Middle East midday heat and sun. The heat didn't stop Jesus from waiting patiently for the Samaritan woman. When He met her, He asked her for a drink of water. To say that the woman of Samaria was a bit surprised by His presence as well as by His request is probably a major understatement. Saint John writes: "The Samaritan woman said to him, 'How is it that you, a Jew, ask a drink of me, a woman of Samaria?' For Jews have no dealing with Samaritans. Jesus answered her, 'If you knew the gift of God, and who it is that is saying to you, "Give me a drink," you would have asked him and he would have given you living water'" (Jn 4:9–10).

Later, the apostles came back and witnessed the exchange going on between Jesus and the Samaritan woman. "Just then his disciples came. They marveled that he was talking with a woman, but none said, 'What do you wish?' or, 'Why are you talking with her?'" (Jn 4:27).

The Samaritan woman knew all too well that Jews and Samaritans didn't get along or associate with each other. The Samaritans were a mixed race of Jewish and pagan heritage and were considered by the Jews to be "unclean". She also knew that men, in general, weren't in the habit of hanging out in the local town square and having deep conversations with women. At first she didn't know quite what to make of Jesus—neither did the apostles, as John Paul II stresses in *Mulieris Dignitatem*:

> It is universally admitted—even by people with a critical attitude towards the Christian message—that *in the eyes of his contemporaries Christ became a promoter of women's true dignity* and of the *vocation* corresponding to this dignity. At times this caused wonder, surprise, often to the point of scandal: "They marvelled that He was talking with a woman", because this behaviour differed from that of his contemporaries. Even Christ's own disciples "marvelled".[2]

Jesus broke the norms. So the obvious conclusion is that if He had wanted to make women apostles or priests, He would have done so, because He wasn't afraid of the reaction. Frankly, the mere suggestion that Jesus was limited by

---

[2] *Mulieris Dignitatem: On the Dignity and Vocation of Women* (August 15, 1988), 12, Holy See website, http://www.vatican.va/holy_father/john_paul_ii/apost_letters/documents/hf_jp-ii_apl_15081988_mulieris-dignitatem_en.html. Emphasis in original.

the times in which He lived drives me nuts. We are talking about God here! How could the Alpha and the Omega, the great "I AM", be limited by the world that He created? It makes no sense. This exchange between Jesus and the woman of Samaria, as well as the Lord's interaction with women at key points in His ministry, shows how He truly valued the contributions of women.

In section 13 of *Mulieris Dignitatem*, John Paul II highlights other important encounters and relationships that clearly illustrate Jesus' recognition of women and the important role they play in the Kingdom of God:

> As we scan the pages of the Gospel, many women, of different ages and conditions, pass before our eyes. We meet women with illnesses or physical sufferings. . . .
>
> Sometimes the women whom Jesus met and who received so many graces from him, also accompanied him as he journeyed with the Apostles through the towns and villages, proclaiming the Good News of the Kingdom of God; and they "provided for them out of their means". . . . Sometimes women appear in the parables which Jesus of Nazareth used to illustrate for his listeners the truth about the Kingdom of God. . . . In all of Jesus' teaching, as well as in his behaviour, one can find nothing which reflects the discrimination against women prevalent in his day. On the contrary, his words and works always express the respect and honour due to women. . . . This way of speaking to and about women, as well as his manner of treating them, clearly constitutes an "innovation" with respect to the prevailing custom at that time.

I am not sure how someone reading the Gospels could come away with something negative about Jesus' relationship with women or get the impression that Jesus oppressed women merely because He did not choose them as apostles. Then again, when I think of my own hardness of heart in the past, I get it. When we want something, we can be like little children who drop to the ground kicking and screaming, demanding that candy bar or toy. We have tunnel vision and are focused on what we think will make us happy.

That analogy is an appropriate one for those supporting women's ordination in the Catholic Church. They see the priesthood as that candy bar that they simply cannot live without. It's their final frontier—the last glass ceiling that needs to be cracked wide open. Women can't possibly have equality in the Church without being allowed to be priests, they say. Since women have practically no limitations any longer in the secular world in terms of career choices and opportunities, some think that the same should be true in the Catholic Church. After all, women can be doctors, lawyers, astronauts, firefighters, and police officers. So why can't we be Catholic priests? However, the Church is not Wall Street or Main Street. The Church is not a democracy; it is a kingdom, as in the Kingdom of God.

It is very difficult for us democratic and equality-minded Americans to understand kingship. A king as a symbol of divine authority has lost all of its meaning. For that matter, many of the symbols that God uses to speak to us about His plan for mankind are no longer understood, beginning with the very fundamental symbols of manhood and womanhood. What does is it mean to be a man? What does it mean to be a woman? Are husbands and wives the same things? Are fathers and mothers? If we have difficulty answering such questions, no wonder so many of us are confused about the priesthood.

Jesus was a man, and as a man He made the priestly offering of Himself in atonement for our sins. He was the bridegroom who voluntarily laid down His life for us, His beloved bride. Jesus chose men to be his priests so they could re-present the sacrifice that He both offered and suffered as a man. They are called to love the Church as a husband loves his bride.

Some in the Church are hoping that women's ordination will someday be a reality. That's simply not going to happen. This is not according to yours truly but according to the Church, and right from the top—as in the Chair of Peter. John Paul II, in his 1994 document *Ordinatio Sacerdotalis*, detailed why the teaching on the priesthood cannot be changed.

> In the Apostolic Letter *Mulieris Dignitatem*,[3] I myself wrote in this regard: "In calling only men as his Apostles, Christ acted in a completely free and sovereign manner. In doing so, he exercised the same freedom with which, in all his behavior, he emphasized the dignity and the vocation of women, without conforming to the prevailing customs and to the traditions sanctioned by the legislation of the time."
>
> In fact the Gospels and the Acts of the Apostles attest that this call was made in accordance with God's eternal plan; Christ chose those whom he willed (cf. Mk 3:13–14; Jn 6:70), and he did so in union with the Father, "through the Holy Spirit" (Acts 1:2), after having spent the night in prayer (cf. Lk 6:12). Therefore, in granting admission to the ministerial priesthood, the Church has always acknowledged as a perennial norm her Lord's way of acting in choosing the twelve men whom he made the foundation of his Church (cf. Rev 21:14). These men did not in fact receive only a function which could thereafter be exercised by any member of the Church; rather they were specifically and intimately associated in the mission of the Incarnate Word himself (cf. Mt 10:1, 7–8; 28:16–20; Mk 3:13–16; 16:14–15). The Apostles did the same when they chose fellow workers who would succeed them in their ministry. Also

---

[3] *Mulieris Dignitatem*, 26.

included in this choice were those who, throughout the time of the Church, would carry on the Apostles' mission of representing Christ the Lord and Redeemer.[4]

John Paul II's *Ordinatio Sacerdotalis* is considered to be the final word on the matter of women's ordination. In 1995, then Joseph Cardinal Ratzinger, now Pope Benedict XVI, was head of the Congregation for the Doctrine of the Faith, and acting in this capacity, he stated that the ban on women priests as taught in *Ordinatio Sacerdotalis* was "set forth infallibly".[5]

Although the matter is considered settled, that doesn't mean we should walk away from a deeper understanding of this teaching. If you're still struggling with this issue, reading and prayerfully reflecting on the above documents and Scripture and consulting a good spiritual advisor or director should help you come to peace with the matter. The Blessed Virgin Mary can also help us better understand the special place of women in the Church. As Pope John Paul II pointed out, the fact that she was not a priest has not in any way detracted from her prominence as Mother of the Church and Queen of Heaven.

Ironically, by placing all of their focus on the priesthood and overlooking all of the important ways women serve, and, yes, even lead, in the Church, feminists actually diminish women. In a *Newsweek* 2010 cover story entitled "What Would Mary Do? How Women Can Save the Catholic Church from Its Sins", the Church was again maligned for her "failure" to come out of the Dark Ages and ordain

[4] John Paul II, *Ordinatio Sacerdotalis* (May 22, 1994), 2.
[5] Congregation for the Doctrine of the Faith, "Responsum ad Propositum Dubium concerning the Teaching Contained in *Ordinatio Sacerdotalis*" (October 28, 1995), Holy See website, http://www.vatican.va/roman_curia/congregations/cfaith/documents/rc_con_cfaith_doc_19951028_dubium-ordinatio-sac_en.html.

women.[6] Thank goodness for the excellent response by Sister Mary Ann Walsh, the director of media relations for the United States Conference of Catholic Bishops. In her article, "What Would Mary Do? Don't Ask *Newsweek*", Walsh demonstrated with the following facts that influence in the Church does not depend upon ordination.[7]

- One-quarter of the diocesan positions at the highest levels, such as chancellor and chief financial officer, are held by women.
- The number of women in leadership positions in Catholic dioceses is comparable to that of the women in the U.S. workforce as a whole.
- Women in the Church, such as Mother Teresa of Calcutta, Catherine of Siena, and Teresa of Avila, touched hearts, changed lives, and in some cases even overshadowed popes.
- Major areas of Catholic influence in the United States are in the educational and health systems, where women have taken the lead from the start.

"The presence and the role of women in the life and mission of the Church, although not linked to the ministerial priesthood, remain absolutely necessary and irreplaceable", wrote John Paul II. "As the Declaration *Inter Insigniores* points out, 'the Church desires that Christian women should become fully aware of the greatness of their mission: today their role is of capital importance both for the renewal and

[6] Lisa Miller, "What Would Mary Do? How Women Can Save the Catholic Church from Its Sins", *Newsweek*, April 12, 2010.

[7] Sister Mary Ann Walsh, "What Would Mary Do? Don't Ask *Newsweek*", Monitor (newspaper of the Roman Catholic Diocese of Trenton, N.J.), April 12, 2010, http://www.trentonmonitor.com/Main.asp?SectionID=6&SubSection ID=84&ArticleID=878.

humanization of society and for the rediscovery by believers of the true face of the Church.' " [8]

The Church: Upholding Women's True Dignity

The most significant documents that led to my realizing that the Church upholds women's true dignity were probably John Paul II's *Mulieris Dignitatem*, his 1995 Letter to Women, and his encyclical *Evangelium Vitae*. Those documents, along with my attendance at the 2008 Vatican congress presented by the Pontifical Council for the Laity, brought it all together for me.

As I learned more about Church teaching on women, I experienced an emotional roller coaster ride. Part of me was thrilled to see what the Church and her leaders had to say about women's roles in the world and the body of Christ. But another part of me was furious. Why hadn't I heard any of this before? I might have been able to avoid a lot of pain and some pretty serious problems in my life if I had been exposed to such depth and beauty in terms of better understanding God's plan for women. Granted, some of John Paul II's documents had not yet been issued when I was growing up, but Vatican II had already started bringing much greater attention to the concerns and needs of women at about the same time that radical feminism started to form on the ideological horizon. The emphasis on women came in the Second Vatican Council's closing message, delivered on December 8, 1965, on the feast of the Immaculate Conception.

> And now it is to you that we address ourselves, women of all states—girls, wives, mothers and widows, to you also,

---

[8] John Paul II, *Ordinatio Sacerdotalis*, 2–3. The final quotation is from Congregation for the Doctrine of the Faith, *Inter Insigniores* (October 15, 1976), 6, in AAS [*Acta Apostolicae Sedis*] 69 (1977): 115–16.

consecrated virgins and women living alone—you constitute half of the immense human family. As you know, the Church is proud to have glorified and liberated woman, and in the course of the centuries, in diversity of characters, to have brought into relief her basic equality with man. But the hour is coming, in fact has come, when the vocation of woman is being achieved in its fullness, the hour in which woman acquires in the world an influence, an effect and a power never hitherto achieved. That is why, at this moment when the human race is under-going so deep a transformation, women impregnated with the spirit of the Gospel can do so much to aid mankind in not falling.[9]

In *Mulieris Dignitatem*, *Evangelium Vitae*, and the 1995 Letter to Women, we read phrases such as "feminine genius" and "new feminism".[10] In section 99 of *Evangelium Vitae*, John Paul II encouraged women to reclaim their uniqueness by embracing, rather than rejecting, their feminine identity. "In transforming culture so that it supports life, women occupy a place, in thought and action, which is unique and decisive. It depends on them to promote a 'new feminism' which rejects the temptation of imitating models of 'male domination', in order to acknowledge and affirm the true genius of women in every aspect of the life of society, and overcome all discrimination, violence and exploitation."

Read the Letter to Women, and you would think you were reading a statement from a secular women's rights group. John Paul II issued this document in 1995, right before the United Nations Conference on Women, held in Beijing

[9] "Address of Pope Paul VI to Women" (closing of the Second Vatican Council, December 8, 1965), Holy See website, http://www.vatican.va/holy_father/paul_vi/speeches/1965/documents/hf_p-vi_spe_19651208_epilogo-concilio-donne_en.html.
[10] See *Mulieris Dignitatem*, 30–31; *Evangelium Vitae*, 99; and "Letter of Pope John Paul II to Women", 9–12.

that year. "There is an urgent need to achieve *real equality* in every area: equal pay for equal work, protection for working mothers, fairness in career advancements, equality of spouses with regard to family rights and the recognition of everything that is part of the rights and duties of citizens in a democratic State."[11]

Maybe I am missing something, but that doesn't sound like a Church that is trying to oppress women. And try this on for size: in that same letter, the Pope thanked women— mothers, wives, working women, consecrated women, and "every woman"—for their contributions.[12] On top of that, he publicly and in writing apologized to women for any wrongs done to them by the Church. His 1995 letter also addressed female objectification, discrimination, and modern-day obstacles that keep women from their full potential.

> Unfortunately, we are heirs to a history which has *conditioned* us to a remarkable extent. In every time and place, this conditioning has been an obstacle to the progress of women. Women's dignity has often been unacknowledged and their prerogatives misrepresented; they have often been relegated to the margins of society and even reduced to servitude. This has prevented women from truly being themselves and it has resulted in a spiritual impoverishment of humanity. . . .
>
> Yes, it is time to *examine the past with courage*, to assign responsibility where it is due in a review of the long history of humanity. Women have contributed to that history as much as men and, more often than not, they did so in much more difficult conditions. . . . But even though time may have buried the documentary evidence of those achievements, their beneficent influence can be felt as a force which has shaped the lives of successive generations, right up to

---

[11] "Letter of Pope John Paul II to Women", 4. Emphasis in original.
[12] Ibid., 1–2.

our own. To this great, immense feminine "tradition" humanity owes a debt which can never be repaid. Yet how many women have been and continue to be valued more for their physical appearance than for their skill, their professionalism, their intellectual abilities, their deep sensitivity; in a word, the very dignity of their being!

And what shall we say of the obstacles which in so many parts of the world still keep women from being fully integrated into social, political and economic life? We need only think of how the gift of motherhood is often penalized rather than rewarded, even though humanity owes its very survival to this gift. Certainly, much remains to be done to prevent discrimination against those who have chosen to be wives and mothers.[13]

The Vatican Women's Congress

I can still remember receiving the invitation to the Vatican women's congress. It was late October 2007. I was going through the mail and spotted an envelope with the impressive Vatican seal. I thought to myself, "Okay, this is either really good or really bad. Maybe the Vatican has a web cam in our radio studio and I said something wrong. Could the envelope I am holding contain the details of my excommunication, perhaps?" Instead, I was giddy to see an invitation to the congress! To this day I can quote directly from the letter because I saved it (and practically every other piece of paper or document related to that event): "Our Dicastery would be very pleased if you could be present at this gathering."

And so off I went to Rome in February of the following year. The event was convened to take an in-depth look at the role of women on the twentieth anniversary of *Mulieris*

[13] Ibid., 3–4. Emphasis in original.

Dignitatem. The Vatican congress was on the theme "Woman and Man: The *Humanum* in its Entirety". The main objectives of the conference, according to the organizers, were the following:

- To review the progress made over the past twenty years in the field of the advancement of women and the recognition of their dignity
- To open up a reflection in the light of revelation on the new cultural paradigms and on the difficulties faced by Catholic women in living according to their identity and in collaborating in fruitful reciprocity with men in building up the Church and society
- To remind women of the beauty of the vocation to holiness, encouraging them to respond to it with increasing awareness and, as players in the mission of the Church, to place at the service of the apostolate, family, workplace and culture, all the richness of the feminine "genius" [14]

It was three days jam-packed with panel discussions and seminars given by cardinals, bishops, Bible scholars, sociologists, Church historians, cultural analysts, and pro-life activists. Topics included Jesus of Nazareth; Mary and women in the Gospel and the early Church; Christianity and the advancement of women; how woman and man were created for each other; problems and contemporary cultural trends; women's responsibility and role in building up society and the Church; and the role and mission of women.

I was extremely grateful to God for being invited to the conference as one of some 280 delegates from around the world. But I was extremely frustrated by the realization that

---

[14] "Twenty Years Since *Mulieris Dignitatem*", Pontificio consiglio per i laici, http://www.laici.org/index.php?p=presentazioneDonnaEN.

the majority of women worldwide knew nothing about the conference and even less about the groundbreaking document *Mulieris Dignitatem*, on which the gathering was based. What little coverage the event did receive in the secular press centered on the issue of women's ordination. Of course, nothing of depth concerning Church teaching on the priesthood was covered. The lack of media coverage doesn't take away from the fact that this convention was an important event and another example of the Church's continued effort to help women understand and reach their full potential without losing their female identity. The meeting concluded with a papal audience, during which Pope Benedict XVI explained how, with *Mulieris Dignitatem*, his predecessor wanted to

> deepen the fundamental anthropological truths of man and woman, the equality of their dignity and the unity of both, the well-rooted and profound diversity between the masculine and the feminine and their vocation to reciprocity and complementarity, to collaboration and to communion. This "uni-duality" of man and woman is based on the foundation of the dignity of every person created in the image and likeness of God, who "male and female he created them" (Gen 1:27), avoiding an indistinct uniformity and a dull and impoverishing equality as much as an irreconcilable and conflictual difference.[15]

Pope Benedict warned against certain "cultural and political trends" that attempt to confuse—and in some cases, even wipe out—the differences between the sexes, viewing male and female as a "cultural construct".

[15] "Address of His Holiness Benedict XVI to the Participants in the International Convention on the Theme 'Woman and Man, the *Humanum* in Its Entirety'" (Clementine Hall, the Vatican, February 9, 2008), Holy See website, http://www.vatican.va/holy_father/benedict_xvi/speeches/2008/february/documents/hf_ben-xvi_spe_20080209_donna-uomo_en.html.

It is necessary to recall God's design that created the human being masculine and feminine, with a unity and at the same time an original difference and complimentary. Human nature and the cultural dimension are integrated in an ample and complex process that constitutes the formation of one's own identity, where both dimensions, that of the feminine and that of the masculine, correspond to and complete each other.

Ever since returning from the meeting, many of the delegates and presenters have been doing their best to share what they learned. I have had the opportunity to write several major articles on the event and incorporate this new insight into many of my presentations. The Pontifical Council for the Laity continues to communicate with attendees as well as address the issues raised in 2008 through additional writings.

Jesus and the Church: The World's Biggest Women's Libbers

One of my favorite analysts and Catholic teachers is Mary Ann Glendon, a former U.S. ambassador to the Vatican. She is a hero of mine for many reasons, including her polite but firm stance against the University of Notre Dame for inviting proabortion president Barack Obama to give the commencement address in 2009. Glendon is an author, a law professor at Harvard, and a sought-after commentator on bioethics and Church related issues. In a brilliant piece for *Crisis* magazine first published in 1997, entitled "The Pope's New Feminism", Glendon challenged those who see the Church as an archaic and discriminatory institution that stifles women.[16] Glendon reminded her readers of the ways

---

[16] "The Pope's New Feminism", *Crisis* 15, no. 3 (March 1997): 28–31. Reprinted online by the Catholic Education Resource Center, http://www.catholiceducation.org/articles/feminism/fe0004.html.

Christianity has helped women. For instance, continental European policies protecting mothers and children were influenced heavily by Catholic social thought, and the wide acceptance of the ideal of permanent monogamy in formerly polygamous cultures is due to Christian influence.

Glendon also took an honest look at a perfect Church run by imperfect human beings. In doing so, she quoted Catholic novelist Flannery O'Connor. The quote is from an exchange O'Connor had with a feminist friend who did her best to point out all of the Church's shortcomings.

> What you actually seem to demand is that the Church put the kingdom of heaven on earth right here now.... Christ was crucified on earth and the Church is crucified in time, and the Church is crucified by all of us, by her members most particularly, because she is a Church of sinners. Christ never said that the Church would be operated in a sinless or intelligent way, but that it would not teach error. This does not mean that each and every priest won't teach error, but that the whole Church speaking through the Pope will not teach error in matters of faith. The Church is founded on Peter who denied Christ three times and couldn't walk on the water by himself. You are expecting his successors to walk on the water.[17]

In closing, Mary Ann Glendon helped us realize that there is no place in contemporary society where a woman is more respected, supported, or encouraged than in the Church. "Neither can I think of any more fruitful principles to guide and promote further progress for women than those contained in Scripture and the Church's social teachings. In particular, the implications of combining John Paul II's

---

[17] Flannery O'Connor to Cecil Dawkins, December 9, 1958, in *The Habit of Being: Letters of Flannery O'Connor*, ed. Sally Fitzgerald (New York: Farrar, Straus and Giroux), p. 307.

writings on women with his writings on family, the laity, human work, and social justice are truly revolutionary—and for the most part yet to be explored. These great writings stand open to the future." [18]

I think we can easily say that since that article was written nearly fifteen years ago, the future is now. Scripture, the writings of John Paul II, and the teachings of the Church are timeless. If we are willing and open, we can continue to unpack them and learn from them. If we do, we will see that Jesus is, and always has been, our biggest fan. He is absolutely the biggest women's libber who ever walked the face of the earth! Nowhere else will a woman find her true identity than in the arms of Christ and the breathtakingly beautiful teachings of our one, holy, catholic, and apostolic faith.

It's important for me to reiterate that as I studied my way back into the faith, part of me was very thrilled, while another part of me was furious. Where had I been all of those years? Why didn't anyone tell me of these teachings? I felt like the folks in the old vegetable juice commercial who smack themselves in the head and proclaim, "Wow, I could've had a V8!" I had to go through what I call a "cultural detox". I had to rid myself of all of my old ways and ideas. I had to put on the mind of Christ and see myself—and the Church—very differently.

Little by little, step by step, the Lord walked me through the Scriptures and the teachings and showed me that the role He has for me and other women is not minimized or less important because we can't be, for example, ordained to the priesthood. I came to see how the role of women was fulfilled not only in physical motherhood—thus bringing into stark relief the devastating consequences that

[18] Glendon, "Pope's New Feminism".

contraception and abortion have on women and society—
but in spiritual motherhood as well. In the Church, I could
find out who I was meant to be in Christ; and, as the great
saint and Doctor of the Church Catherine of Siena said,
"When we are whom we are called to be, we will set the
world ablaze."

With the help of Christ along with the teachings of the
Church, you too can set the world on fire. What are you
waiting for?

Questions for Reflection

1. Over the years, what has been your impression
    or understanding of the Church and her treat-
    ment of women?
2. What has been your general understanding of Jesus
    in terms of His efforts to promote true dignity
    for women?
3. Is there a particular passage in the New Testa-
    ment regarding women in the life of Christ that
    really speaks to your heart?
    * The Woman at the Well: John 4:1–42
    * Jesus anointed at Bethany: Matthew 26:6–12;
      John 12:1–8; Luke 7:37
    * Martha and Mary: Luke 10:38–42
    * Adulterous Woman: John 8:1–3
4. What issues pertaining to women in the Church
    have been challenging for you?
5. What are your thoughts about the "new femi-
    nism" and "feminine genius"?

Chapter 7

Extreme Media Makeover

Your Personal Media Reality Check and Spiritual Beauty Plan

Look to him, and be radiant;
so your faces shall never be ashamed.

—Psalm 34:5

If we truly desire to find out what God has in store for us, then we must, as the subtitle of this book suggests, allow ourselves to be transformed by Christ instead of conformed to the culture—and that means an *extreme* media makeover, or a cultural detox, as I like to call it. The culture can be toxic in terms of desensitizing us to violence, weakening our moral fiber, and making us feel pretty darn disgusted with ourselves because we're not five foot nine and a size 2. So how do we get started? How do we start shedding old ideas and thoughts that may be contrary to Church teaching and start putting on the mind of Christ? Well, consider this chapter your own spiritual spa—you're going to walk in, sit down, and have some work done. When your makeover is finished, you'll walk out of the spiritual spa refreshed and renewed with some great "products" in hand. Inside the spiritual spa goodie bag, which in this case is this particular chapter, you'll find your own personal spiritual beauty plan, including a long list of activities, resources, and guidelines to help you maintain healthier habits that can be used to strengthen your relationship with God as well as boost your self-esteem.

See Yourself First and Foremost as a Daughter of the King

Jesus is the King of Kings and Lord of Lords. We are his children. If He is King, then that makes you a princess and His daughter. I don't care how rough things may be in your life right now; embrace this thought about being a child of God who has great dignity and worth just because you are you. Write this down and repeat it at least once a day: "I am a daughter of the King." This is where the spiritual makeover begins. We have to love ourselves before we can love anyone else. As it says in Psalm 139: "For you formed my inward parts, you knitted me together in my mother's womb. I praise you, for I am wondrously made. Wonderful are your works!" (vv. 13–14).

God doesn't make junk. Never forget that. Stop taking your body image cues from images in magazines. No one looks like the models on the pages of *Glamour* or *InStyle*, even the models themselves. Their flaws are hidden through great photography, lighting, computerized imaging, professional makeup artists, and in many cases plastic surgery.

Don't take your cues for personal and professional success, as well as how to be a good mother, from the media either. Again I have to say, "Been there, done that, and bought the T-shirt." Something has to give when we try to be everything to everyone all the time or to "have it all". It doesn't work. Something—or someone—will suffer. That's why it is so important to achieve balance. Even some of the Christian magazines set the bar unusually high for women and can make us feel like failures. Don't you just love the images around Christmastime of the families in matching festive outfits sitting at the most beautifully set tables, happily waiting to say their prayers and then dive into the Norman Rockwell-like spread before them? That simply is not reality, at least not with most of the families I know.

Some of the best feedback I ever received on one of my *Our Sunday Visitor* columns had to do with avoiding what I call the "super-Catholic syndrome".[1] In this particular column, I wrote with great affection and admiration about a cousin of mine who came up with a great idea in a snap—an idea that saved her youngest on his school Christmas goodie day and quickly became a family and parish school tradition. My cousin, a working mom with four children, had forgotten to make Christmas cookies for her youngest son's class. Of course, she didn't realize the faux pas until the morning of goodie day, just as she was frantically trying to get all the children dressed, fed, and out the door. She did remember, thanks be to God, that she had a few boxes of Little Debbie Swiss Cake Rolls stashed in the cupboard. She grabbed the packages, along with some confectioner's sugar, green icing, and red candies—all the supplies she was going to use to make those perfect cookies for goodie day—and created a show stopper. "Sprigs" of green icing topped by a red candy served as her version of holly, and with a little sprinkle of confectioner's sugar, voilà—miniature Christmas Yule logs were born! (The folks on the Food Network would be so proud.)

Of course, this is not to knock the homemade or the personal touch. But we have to be realistic. Sometimes we

---

[1] "Christmas Composure", *Our Sunday Visitor*, December 13, 2009, http://www.osv.com/tabid/7621/itemid/5712/Christmas-composure.aspx.

have to let go of having the picture-perfect whatever in order to concentrate on what's really important. What mattered to my cousin was not letting her son down and living up to a commitment she had made. While her treats didn't come out of her oven, they came from her heart. She used her God-given ingenuity to create a big smile on her son's face as well as the faces of many a teacher and a student that Christmas. Do your best, but do yourself a big favor: stop comparing yourself to others, especially to the images in the media. And remember: you are a daughter of the King!

Cheryl Dickow, my dear friend and the publisher of *Newsflash!*, my personal testimony book (mentioned in chapter 4), shares an honest story about her efforts one Halloween to be that "perfect" mom who bakes and sews. Sewing was not—and is not—one of Cheryl's God-given gifts, but she wanted to give her son the best Halloween costume ever! Her plan: shred a few white sheets and wrap her son in such a way that he would be a mummy. A little nip here, a tuck there, a bit of glue, some thread and a needle, a staple, a bit of rope—no matter what she tried, Cheryl could not figure out how to get the darn costume to stay up. Finally, she let her son out the door, encouraging him that he really did look like a mummy as the sheets slowly slipped off his body and dragged on the ground. By the fourth house, the boy was no longer attired in his mummy costume, and both mother and son were overcome with laughter, each appreciating the other's predicament.

I love that story because it is the quintessential reminder that none of us is perfect but that even in our imperfection we are loved by Christ—we are His daughters. Like the improvised Little Debbie Yule logs, the mummy costume becomes so much more than a failed attempt at something; rather, it is an on-the-nose reminder of what really matters in our lives as wives, mothers, friends, and daughters.

Receive the Sacrament of Reconciliation Regularly

God loves us right where we are at, but He also loves us too much to leave us there. In other words, if we are still walking the earth, God isn't done with us yet. This life is a journey, a pilgrimage that in the end, God willing, will bring us to heaven. Many women, however, are stuck in one spot along the road. They can't progress in their relationship or walk with God because they believe they can never measure up or that their past sins can never be forgiven. They're carrying way too heavy of a load of guilt and unworthiness. That's the evil one trying to keep you away from God and especially the confessional. I heard the well-known Evangelical preacher Joyce Meyer say once, "The devil will convince you that sin is no big deal, and then when you do sin, he will never let you forget it."

Now, if you're at the spa getting a facial, the first thing the technician will do is remove your makeup. Then she might do some deep cleansing and moisturizing. The spiritual version of this is to start with the Sacrament of Reconciliation. Going to Confession once a month is a good way to start fresh and to wipe away any sins you might be carrying from the past. Most of us can't afford a fancy facial every month. The good news about Confession is that it's free, and the results last a lot longer than a mud masque or a skin peel!

One of the most powerful spiritual experiences I ever had happened during Confession. It was the last week of Lent and since our parish in suburban Detroit is so large, our pastor brought in several priests to assist in offering the Sacrament. I had already confessed the major mortal sins in my life, including the use of contraception and promiscuity, but for some reason I did not feel forgiven. Having different priests come to our parish gave me the option of going to a priest I didn't know, and I quickly took advantage of that opportunity. I didn't do any reconfessing but I talked to the priest about some venial sins that kept reoccurring. I noticed that his eyes were closed, and he seemed to be really listening to me and at the same time to be in deep prayer and thought. When I finished, he opened his eyes, and as if he were looking straight into my soul he asked, "Why don't you see yourself as a loved daughter of God?" I was stunned. I received my penance, walked back to the pew in a daze, and then started to cry. I realized that I had just experienced the priest acting *in persona Christi*, that is, the priest was speaking for Christ. How else could the priest know something that was so deep in the corners of my heart? Through the priest, Jesus was telling me to let go of the past and know that I had long been forgiven.

Never doubt the power of Confession. Don't be concerned about the process if you haven't been to the Sacrament in a while. The priest will walk you through the steps. But here are a few suggestions:

1. Before you go to Confession, examine your conscience to determine what mortal or venial sins you may have committed.

2. The Ten Commandments offer a great opportunity for reflection before going to receive this Sacrament. Review them in prayer before entering the confessional.

3. Once entering the confessional, make the Sign of the Cross and say, "Bless me, Father, for I have sinned. It has been [amount of time] since my last Confession." Then tell the priest your sins.

4. The priest might talk to you a little before giving you a penance to perform—an act of love by which you can make some amends for your sins. Before giving absolution or forgiveness for your sins, the

priest might ask you to recite an act of contrition. Here is one I like to use:

> O my God, I am heartily sorry
> For having offended Thee,
> and I detest all my sins,
> because I dread the loss of heaven,
> and the pains of hell;
> but most of all because
> they offend Thee, my God,
> Who are all good and
> deserving of all my love.
> I firmly resolve,
> with the help of Thy grace,
> to confess my sins,
> to do penance,
> and to amend my life.
> Amen.

5. After the priest forgives and dismisses you, do your penance as soon as possible.

It sounds too good to be true, doesn't it? We commit major sins—and all fall short, as Saint Paul tells us in the letter to the Romans—yet God is always there ready to give us another chance, ready to grab the cotton balls and the astringent and wipe away the dirt and grime.

Confession—it's good for the soul, and a definite must in our spiritual makeover.

Make a Concerted Effort to Silence the Noise in Your Life

On the cover of my first book, *Noise: How Our Media-Saturated Culture Dominates Lives and Dismantles Families* (mentioned in chapter 1), I have a thought-provoking quote from

Pope Benedict XVI: "We are no longer able to hear God. There are too many different frequencies filling our ears." [2]

Think about that. The first thing we should be doing when we awaken is get down on our knees or bow our heads in a prayer of thanksgiving for another day. Instead, most of us hop out of bed and turn on the TV, the radio, or both. Many also hop on the Internet to check e-mail and turn on their cell phones to start calling or texting a friend or a co-worker about this, that, or the other thing. Given the fact that, as we discussed in chapter 2, children are using media on average fifty-three hours a week,[3] it's not a stretch to say that your son or daughter is probably online or in front of the television set before leaving for school. So you have all the noise from the media plus the inherent noise of one of the busiest parts of the day coming at you full speed ahead—noise, noise, and more noise. We rush to work and to school with the radio blaring and the cell phone ringing, and before we know it, the day is well under way and we haven't even taken time to hear what God has to say to us. Then we get angry with God or frustrated when life doesn't go our way. We have to silence the noise in our lives if we want to hear from God and live a more peaceful and less stressful life. Blessed Teresa of Calcutta said that God cannot be found in noise and restlessness: "God is the friend of silence. . . . See how nature, the trees, the flowers, the grass grow in deep silence. See how the stars, the moon and the sun move in silence. . . . We need this silence in order to touch souls." [4]

---

[2] Homily (outdoor site of the Neue Messe, Munich, September 10, 2006), Holy See website, http://www.vatican.va/holy_father/benedict_xvi/homilies/2006/documents/hf_ben-xvi_hom_20060910_neue-messe-munich_en.html.

[3] See p. 40–41.

[4] Susan Conroy, *Mother Teresa's Lessons of Love and Secrets of Sanctity* (Huntington, Ind.: Our Sunday Visitor, 2003), p. 120.

In the Old Testament, we see how God spoke to Elijah on Mount Horeb. God was actually passing by Elijah. Since it's the great "I AM" we are talking about here, you might think that God would make Himself known to Elijah with some very dramatic act of nature. That's not what happened.

> And behold, the LORD passed by, and a great and strong wind tore the mountains, and broke in pieces the rocks before the LORD, but the LORD was not in the wind; and after the wind an earthquake, but the LORD was not in the earthquake; and after the earthquake a fire, but the LORD was not in the fire; and after the fire a still small voice. And when Elijah heard it, he wrapped his face in his mantle and went out and stood at the entrance of the cave (1 Kings 19: 11–13).

The transforming experience I had when I finally silenced myself, when I stopped talking and listened to what God was trying to say to me about my future, is worth repeating. It was toward the end of my secular television news career. I had become very frustrated with the news business. Since I was back in the Church with a passion, I believed that the Lord would continue to use me as a Christian in the secular media. My calling, or so I thought at the time, was to shine the light of Christ in the newsroom. That wasn't working out very well because the news business was becoming increasingly sensational and biased; the news executives weren't buying what I was selling, and it was very confusing. One evening, as I was home preparing dinner, I cried out to God and asked Him to please show me what I was supposed to do with my life. It's important to note that there was no TV or radio on at the time. It was just me, my sniffles, and God. After I had a good crying and whining session, I quieted myself down and continued cooking dinner. That's when the words "I can't use you in the secular media anymore" came to me. The words were so clear that they seemed like they were from an audible voice in the room. What would have happened if I had been on the phone or watching TV?

This is where our "media reality check" enters the picture. Silencing some of the noise in your life will help you in your prayer life and allow you, as well as your family, to have some beneficial quiet time. Wouldn't it be nice just to walk into the house and not have to shout over the television? When was the last time you ate dinner with your family without some interference from modern media technology? This media reality check, if you're honest with yourself, will help you and your loved ones assess just how much time you spend watching TV or "friending" people on Facebook. It will help you detox in terms of learning to limit the amount of time spent with media. The media is a great tool for evangelization, communication, and faith education; unfortunately, most Catholics are not spending their media time listening to Catholic radio or visiting Catholic websites. That's why most of us can benefit from applying a media reality check:

- Build a "media-free zone" into your daily routine at home or at work. Silence the noise and allow yourself quiet time (start with fifteen to thirty minutes) with God.
- Take control of the media outlets in your home by taking TVs and computers out of the bedrooms (including yours) and putting them in a central area that allows regular monitoring.
- Set and keep media guidelines in terms of time limits. The American Academy of Pediatrics recommends no more than two hours a day of TV for children in grade school and high school, and no TV for children younger than two years of age.[5]

[5] American Academy of Pediatrics Committee on Public Education, "Children, Adolescents, and Television", *Pediatrics* 107, no. 2 (February 2001).

- Keep family meals completely media free. Turn off the TV and the cell phones. Let voice mail handle your calls.
- Don't make the TV or the computer the main focal point of your home.
- Think WWJW, or what would Jesus watch? Spending time soaking up movies or TV programs loaded with sexual or violent content is offensive to God and offensive to your spirit.

What we take in from the media on a regular basis can impact our thoughts and our behavior. Garbage in, garbage out, is the best way to put it. That means that our media habits, if they're more negative than positive, could lead to our not taking our faith or our time with God as seriously. Conducting a media reality check at least once or twice a year can really boost that spiritual makeover and make it last for a long time to come. Advent and Lent are great liturgical seasons to do this. If you have children, why not make the media reality check a family event? This will help instill solid habits in your children, habits that just might prevent them from needing a major spiritual makeover later in life.

Remember that the Blessed Mother Is Watching You

This is a phrase I used to hear quite often from my very wise and shrewd Italian American mother, usually when I was heading out the door to go on a date. Pretty sharp, that mother of mine. She figured a little Italian Catholic guilt never hurt anyone. And it worked, at least while I was still living at home. If I was about to do something I knew deep down was wrong, I would hear that voice and think twice.

Looking back now, and after having many a conversation with my mother about this particular expression, I realize that she was also trying to help me remember the important role the Blessed Mother and the saints have in our lives. The Blessed Mother is watching you and me because she is our Mother. She is our advocate and intercessor and is always pointing us toward her Son. One of the unfortunate developments after the Second Vatican Council was the loss in some Catholic circles of some types of formal prayer, including the Rosary. I don't know about you, but I had eight years of Catholic grade school, and I never learned how to pray the Rosary. I taught myself after my return to the Church. Thank goodness you just can't keep a good lady down, as in our Lady. The Rosary has made a major comeback. If you're not in the habit of praying the Rosary, give it a try—or another try, as the case may be. It is a very peaceful and meaningful form of prayer. You can find a Rosary instruction manual by doing a quick search online;[6] most Catholic bookstores will also have them.

The Blessed Mother and the communion of saints— what a gift. It's an army of soul sisters and brothers interceding for us before the throne of God. Devotion to the saints is another one of those timeless tools that can really pack quite a spiritual punch and enhance our spiritual beauty. Think about it this way: if you're having a day at the spa, you're probably not alone—you most likely have a friend along for the encouragement and the experience. Asking for one of the great saints to intercede for you is like having a spiritual spa companion along to help you on the road to holiness. One of my favorite books on intercession

---

[6] You can find instructions for how to pray the Rosary at the following websites: http://www.ewtn.com/faith/teachings/maryd5.htm; http://www.catholic.com/library/Rosary.asp; or http://www.catholic.org/prayers/rosary.php.

of the Blessed Mother and the saints is written by apologist Patrick Madrid, *Any Friend of God's Is a Friend of Mine*.[7] It's considered one of the best explanations regarding the Catholic doctrine on the communion of saints, so I highly recommend it.

Two of my all-time favorite saints are female Doctors of the Church: Saint Teresa of Avila and Saint Catherine of Siena. I was actually named after Saint Teresa of Avila, which led to my doing a great deal of research on her life. Saint Teresa is considered one of the great mystics. She lived in the sixteenth century, at the time of the Protestant Reformation. She is a great example of someone who was all about the spiritual beauty plan and extreme makeover. She was the reformer of the Carmelite order and was known for her Counter-Reformation work defending the Catholic Church. She wrote extensively on contemplative prayer and spiritual development, which was based a great deal on her experience of reforming her life. I love Saint Teresa not just for her contributions to the Church in the area of spiritual growth—which are incredible—but for her very direct way of speaking to Jesus and for her often-whimsical way of speaking about life in general. Once, when she was having a particularly rough day, she looked up at the heavens and said, "Lord, if this is the way You treat your friends, no wonder You have so few." Saint Teresa even compared life on earth, with all of its trials and tribulations, to "a night in a bad inn". She also struggled with many of the same temptations women deal with today, including materialism. She loved to dance and had no time for whiners. "Lord, preserve us from sour-faced saints."

My second favorite saint, Saint Catherine of Siena, could be called the makeover expert, especially when it comes to

[7] *Any Friend of God's Is a Friend of Mine: A Biblical and Historical Explanation of the Catholic Doctrine of the Communion of Saints* (San Diego: Basilica Press, 1996).

the Church hierarchy. This patron saint of Italy challenged princes of the Church and entire principalities in her short thirty-three years on earth. You think we have issues in the Church today? What Saint Catherine witnessed as far as corruption in the Catholic Church makes present-day scandals look like a walk in the park.

When she was six years old, she had a vision of Christ seated in glory with Saint Peter, Saint Paul, and Saint John that set her vocation in motion. Catherine experienced what she referred to in her letters as a "mystical marriage" to Christ. She eventually became known as a worker of miracles. She is credited with bringing the papacy back to Rome from France in the late fourteenth century following the Great Schism. She is considered a theologian and a philosopher. I'm still working my way through her writings, including *The Dialogue* (or *Treatise on Divine Providence*), but have really enjoyed biographies on the saint, including Sigrid Undset's *Catherine of Siena*.[8]

Granted, I doubt if most of us could ever come at all close to achieving the level of holiness attained by the likes of Saint Teresa and Saint Catherine. This shouldn't stop us, though, from getting to know them and learning from them. I have called on their help countless times since my reversion to the Church. Consider their intercession, or the intercession of any of our great Catholic saints, as the "deluxe" spiritual spa treatment!

Brush Up on Your Catholicism

This is where the media, when used wisely, can be a real friend and not a foe. There has been no other time in the

---

[8] *Catherine of Siena* (New York: Sheed and Ward, 1954 / San Francisco: Ignatius Press, 2009).

history of the Catholic Church that learning about our faith has been easier. With all of the technological resources, including Catholic radio and TV, Catholic websites, podcasts, Catholic networking sites, blogs, and so forth, there is simply no reason not to know your faith. With the click of a mouse, you can be on the relatively new Vatican website www.news.va and be transported to Rome. This website is a collection of all the major stories from the Church herself, not the secular press. You can also watch recent videos of the Pope, read his weekly statements from the General Audience and the Angelus, check out the latest news in the Vatican newspaper, *L'Osservatore Romano*, and much more. The Pope even has his own YouTube page, www.pope2you.net. You can learn to defend the faith by visiting the Catholic Answers website (www.catholic.com) or by watching EWTN, the Eternal World Television Network (www.ewtn.com). You can find out the latest developments with the U.S. bishops by visiting their website (www.usccb.org). You can read reflections from top Catholic thinkers and writers by visiting such online resources as Ignatius Insight (www.ignatiusinsight.com) and the website for *Inside the Vatican* magazine (www.insidethevatican.com).

How about tuning out the local news-talk, country music, or shock jock station and instead tuning into Catholic radio on your way to work? With 170 affiliates around the country, plus online and satellite radio stations (Sirius 130), there is a Catholic radio outlet near you filling the airwaves and your ears with positive and uplifting programming. Catholic radio in particular is near and dear to my heart, of course, as I have been blessed to host a daily morning talk show, *Catholic Connection with Teresa Tomeo*, produced by Ave Maria Radio and syndicated through EWTN. Catholic radio is helping to evangelize, or reevangelize, the country, according to a major survey conducted by Immaculate Heart Radio, based in California. Immaculate Heart Radio operates twenty-four stations serving northern and central California, New Mexico, Reno, Salt Lake City, and Phoenix. In the poll, commissioned in 2010, the network discovered that it had a bigger effect on people than it realized, according to Doug Sherman, founder and president.

> We knew we were having an impact on people. We get calls and emails all the time thanking us for being on the air. Over the years we've heard from literally thousands of people who tell us that our programming has brought them back to the Church, or closer to God, or strengthened their marriage. But we had no idea what a profound difference our stations were having on local parishes. It's truly humbling![9]

The radio network conducted an online survey of nearly two thousand listeners and found the following:

- 94 percent of listeners were more spiritually engaged and inspired.
- 69 percent were better able to teach their children about the truths of the Church.
- 47 percent attended Mass more frequently.
- 51 percent were more involved in and more generous to their local parish.
- 12 percent had their marriages saved.

That's quite a testimony for what media, when used wisely, can do. There is also the ripple effect to consider—just one person excited and knowledgeable about his faith becomes an evangelist, and the possibilities are, frankly, endless.

[9] Immaculate Heart Radio, "Survey Reveals Impact of Immaculate Heart Radio on Parish Life", news release, December 13, 2010, http://ihradio.com/about-2/survey-results/.

The moral of the story: learn about your faith. We will all eventually have to answer for what we know. In this day and age of information technology, it's getting harder and harder to feign ignorance.

Remember that Ignorance of Scripture Is Ignorance of Christ

Speaking of ignorance or "playing dumb", not knowing the Bible is not a wise move, according to Saint Jerome. He said, "Ignorance of Scripture is ignorance of Christ." Saint Jerome is a Father and a Doctor of the Catholic Church who was also a great Bible scholar. He is best known for his translation of the Bible into Latin, which came to be known as the Vulgate.

What Saint Jerome says is very serious. The Bible, after all, is our love letter from God Himself. If we are in a relationship with someone, we communicate with that person. We send e-mails, presents, and cards. We look forward to talking with him on the phone or receiving a text from him. Well, if we love God, don't we want to hear what He has to say to us?

This again is where modern technology is on our side. Since 1996, there has been an explosion of solid Catholic Bible study materials. The availability of good resources wasn't always the case; for far too long, where organized Bible studies were concerned, Protestant studies were the norm. I will be forever grateful for my Protestant friends who gave me and my husband a greater appreciation for Scripture—as I mentioned in chapter 1, my husband came back to the Church through a Protestant Bible study. However, it's important for Catholics to study and read the Bible from a Catholic perspective; otherwise, you miss much about the Eucharist, the Blessed Mother, and the saints, as well as other core Catholic teachings, especially regarding Baptism and salvation.

There are a number of excellent Catholic Bible studies taking place around the country. One of my favorites is *Catholic Scripture Study*.[10] This study includes programs written by Bible experts such as convert and apologist Steve Ray. *Catholic Scripture Study* and most of the other studies involve a weekly two- to three-hour class with take-home questions. I was enrolled in *Catholic Scripture Study* for several years and highly recommend it.

If you don't have time to join a weekly class, you should at least be reading Scripture daily. Scripture reading and reflection is a great way to connect with God, learn more about the saints and their feast days, and get a better understanding of the ebb and flow of the Church's liturgical seasons. I guarantee that once you get into the habit of diving into the daily Mass readings, it will begin to seem as if the Lord is moving those readings around just to address something happening in your life. Daily Catholic devotionals based on the readings of the Mass, and most include reflections from the saints and Catholic writers. Many devotionals are available online; for example, see the website for *The Word among Us* magazine (www.wau.org). The website of the U.S. Conference of Catholic Bishops (www.usccb.org) includes a video reflection on the day's Scripture. Hard copies of devotionals are also available; *Magnificat* is a wonderful scriptural tool (see their website at www.magnificat.net). *The Word among Us* also comes in a print version.

When you love someone, you want to keep in touch with him. Jesus is waiting to speak to us in His Word. He's right there in that Bible which may be gathering dust on

---

[10] Materials are available from the Catholic Scripture Study, Inc., website, www.catholicscripturestudyinc.org.

the shelf or the coffee table. He is just waiting to communicate and be in a relationship with you. As a former pastor of mine once said, "Think of the Bible as an acronym: basic instructions before leaving earth!" A daily dose of the Bible is definitely something we want to throw in our spiritual makeover goodie bag.

When It Comes to the News Media, Consider the Source

When it comes to coverage of the Catholic Church, I wouldn't give the secular media—with the exception of maybe the *Wall Street Journal*, the *National Review*, the Fox News Channel, and a few conservative news-talk radio programs—much consideration at all. To quote another one of our wonderful bishops, Samuel Aquila, of Fargo, North Dakota: "Do not depend on the media for your understanding of what Pope Benedict XVI states, rather go to the source in order to find truth and not someone's misunderstanding and false interpretation." [11]

This quote from Bishop Aquila was part of a statement released November 22, 2010, just days after a media frenzy erupted over comments made by the Pope regarding condom usage. The comments were made in *Light of the World: The Pope, the Church, and the Signs of the Times*, a beautiful book that was the result of an exclusive interview with Pope Benedict XVI by Catholic convert and journalist Peter Seewald. [12] Among the many questions Seewald posed were several relating to the Church's teaching on contraception. As

---

[11] "Bishop Samuel Aquila Responds to False Interpretation of the Words of Pope Benedict XVI", news release, November 22, 2010, http://www.zenit.org/article-31041?l=english.

[12] Peter Seewald and Benedict XVI, *Light of the World: The Pope, the Church, and the Signs of the Times* (San Francisco: Ignatius Press, 2010).

Bishop Aquila went on to explain, the media totally misinterpreted and incorrectly reported what the Holy Father had to say regarding condom usage.

> At issue here are the words of Pope Benedict XVI regarding condom use. The news stories and some of the comments solicited from the public would interpret his words as proclaiming a shift in the Catholic Church's teaching on condom use, and contraception in general. . . . This conclusion is incorrect as can be easily seen by examining the actual text from the book. The Holy Father is not condoning the use of condoms, but making an observation regarding the awakening of a sense of responsibility in the people who are caught up in the habitual sin of prostitution. He does not offer a new moral evaluation of the use of condoms, neither in principle nor practically in this circumstance, but is merely describing a psychological development as one, even in the grip of sin, can begin to acknowledge the safety and human dignity of another.[13]

What actually transpired in the interview? Well, Seewald brought up the topic of the use of condoms in the fight against AIDS. He referred back to comments made on the papal plane on the way to Africa in 2009, when the Pope had said that the only real way to stop the spread of AIDS was to follow traditional Church teaching on sexuality. Seewald noted that many people object to forbidding condom usage for such a high-risk population. Benedict replied:

> There may be a basis in the case of some individuals, as perhaps when a male prostitute uses a condom, where this can be a first step in the direction of a moralization, a first assumption of responsibility, on the way toward recovering

[13] "Bishop Samuel Aquila Responds to False Interpretation".

an awareness that not everything is allowed and that one cannot do whatever one wants. But it is not really the way to deal with the evil of HIV infection. That can really lie only in a humanization of sexuality.[14]

Of course, our sex-crazed media took that to mean that the Church had not only lifted her ban on condom usage (she didn't) but had lifted her ban on contraception altogether (she didn't). In addition to revealing the media's obsession with sex, such a misinterpretation also revealed its ignorance of Church teaching and Church structure. Do journalists really think that such a decision on a core teaching of the Church would be released in a book? The fact that secular news people actually thought that this was the case should give the average Catholic reason not to take his cues on Church teaching from the secular press.

Unfortunately, I heard from many Catholics who were taking the media's version of these developments as Gospel, no pun intended. "How could this be?" one listener asked me in an e-mail. "The Church is finally coming into the twenty-first century", stated yet another listener. And these are folks who listen to Catholic radio. (Just to be clear, the teaching on contraception cannot change; it is an infallible teaching.) A great deal of damage was done by the media's sloppy reporting and sensationalizing of the Holy Father's words. We didn't see or hear the secular press report on how condoms are not fully reliable in terms of preventing HIV transmission. Nor did we read or see stories in the secular press concerning the major decrease in the number of HIV infections in countries such as Uganda where abstinence, not condom use, has been promoted. This is just one blatant example of why we can't

---

[14] Seewald and Benedict XVI, *Light of the World*, p. 119.

trust the majority of the secular press to give us the facts regarding our faith.

I am not saying that you should never watch a secular news program again or that you should cancel all of your subscriptions to secular papers and magazines. I would, however, caution against using the secular media as your main source of news and information—especially when it comes to matters of papal statements and Church teaching. There are a number of great Catholic news sources that provide breaking news on matters both inside and outside the Church, including world events. Such news sources include the following:

Catholic Culture—www.catholicculture.org
Catholic News Agency—www.catholicnewsagency.com
EWTN News—www.ewtnnews.com
Ignatius Insight—www.ignatiusinsight.com
National Catholic Register—www.ncregister.com
Our Sunday Visitor—www.osv.com
Zenit—www.zenit.org

In an address to the American Bible Society in May 2009, archbishop of Philadelphia Charles J. Chaput reminded Catholics of the importance of choosing news sources wisely: "The American news and entertainment media, which now so often overlap, are the largest catechetical syndicate in history.... We can't really know our times until we first know how our mass media work—and especially *how they work on us*.... We can learn to judge them soberly and critically. And if we don't, the consequences may be very unhappy." [15]

[15] "Thoughts on the Mission of St. Paul" (address, American Bible Society, May 6, 2009), http://www.archden.org/index.cfm/ID/2015. Emphasis in original.

Spiritual Beauty Plan: Final Consultation

So we've spent the day at the spiritual spa getting our extreme media makeover. Let's take another look inside our goodie bag and review our spiritual beauty plan.

Spiritual Beauty Plan
- See yourself first and foremost as a daughter of the King.
- Receive the Sacrament of Reconciliation regularly.
- Make a concerted effort to silence the noise in your life.
- Remember that the Blessed Mother is watching you.
- Brush up on your Catholicism.
- Remember that ignorance of Scripture is ignorance of Christ.
- When it comes to the news media, consider the source.

Don't forget to take advantage of the spiritual beauty products that were mentioned; you'll find a review list below. I like to think of these resources as spiritual moisturizer or foundation. You wouldn't step outside without protecting your skin or looking presentable—why not do the same with your soul? These tools will help you in presenting yourself to the Lord.

Information on the Vatican, Church Statements, Teachings, and Documents
Catholic Answers—www.catholic.com
The Holy See—www.vatican.va
Inside the Vatican—www.insidethevatican.com
Pope2You—www.pope2you.net
U.S. Conference of Catholic Bishops—www.usccb.org
Vatican News—www.news.va

Catholic Devotionals and Bible Studies
Catholic Scripture Study—www.catholicscripturestudyinc.org
Magnificat—www.magnificat.net
U.S. Conference of Catholic Bishops—www.usccb.org
The Word among Us—www.wau.org

Reliable Catholic News Sources
Catholic Culture—www.catholicculture.org
Catholic News Agency—www.catholicnewsagency.com
EWTN News—www.ewtnnews.com
Ignatius Insight—www.ignatiusinsight.com
National Catholic Register—www.ncregister.com
Our Sunday Visitor—www.osv.com
Zenit—www.zenit.org

The Catholic Church has so much to offer us. We could spend an entire lifetime studying the Church and only begin to scratch the surface. But we have to start somewhere, and an extreme media makeover is a major step in the right direction. By going through a cultural detox, we can cleanse ourselves of all kinds of junk, noise, and negativity that may be clogging our spiritual pores. We can start fresh with a new focus on what's most important in life: our relationship with Christ and His Church.

There is within our limitations, our faults and failures a divinely conceived creature waiting to be released, waiting to break through to a level of life only God can conceive.

—Attributed to Saint Teresa of Avila

Questions for Reflection

1. In what ways might I be in need of an "extreme media makeover"?

2. Are my media habits leading to vanity, selfishness, poor self-esteem, or relationship problems?

3. Am I truly a servant of the Lord, or am I a woman controlled by the culture and my own worldly desires?

4. Am I taking time to study God's Word and the teachings of His Church?

5. Am I willing to make changes in my life, specifically in media habits that might be hampering my relationship with God?

Chapter 8

Hope Springs Eternal

Encouraging Signs from the Cultural Front Lines

When you say a situation or a person is hopeless,
you are slamming the door in the face of God.

—Charles L. Allen,
All Things Are Possible through Prayer

It's not all gloom and doom. Yes, we certainly have our work
cut out for us, and there are many challenges ahead—but there
is a lot of good news to report from the cultural front lines.
While it's important to have a good understanding of the issues,
it's also nice to get a shot in the arm once in a while and see
that Chicken Little was wrong: although plenty of storm clouds
continue to develop, the sky is not falling.

Church Teachings Are Proven Right Repeatedly

Truth is truth, and it cannot be supressed. Whether we are
talking abortion, contraception, or embryonic stem cell
research, the Church is proven right over and over again. The
world may not want to see it or admit it, but it is important
for us to be able to step back and connect the dots. God's plan

works. The science is on our side. When we go against God's plan or the natural order, we suffer severe consequences. It sounds so simple, and it really is. There is a reason the Ten Commandments are called "commandments" and not "suggestions". Remember this when you are feeling overwhelmed by those trying to convince you otherwise.

You're Not Crazy, and You're Not Alone

Despite what Chris Matthews, Joy Behar, and the rest of the mouthpieces of the secular press want you to think, people of faith and traditional values, by far, represent the majority of American citizens. Carl Anderson, in his most recent book, *Beyond a House Divided: The Moral Consensus Ignored by Washington, Wall Street, and the Media*, gives us an encouraging collection of data showing how—whether it be on the topic of same-sex "marriage", abortion, divorce, health care, or the role of religion in the United States—Americans are united in their beliefs.[1] By a three-to-one margin, Americans think the country needs to return to traditional values. Anderson, the Supreme Knight of the Knights of Columbus, in an interview with the Catholic newsweekly *Our Sunday Visitor*, believes Americans are not as divided as some might think on core issues. "If you're just going with the typical portrait of American public opinion that you see in the media, the country seems to be equally divided on a number of controversial issues. But our political data seemed to suggest that wasn't necessarily the case; that there is actually a consensus on many of the issues that are typically portrayed as most divisive: religion in the public square, abortion, marriage, the role of

[1] *Beyond a House Divided: The Moral Consensus Ignored by Washington, Wall Street, and the Media* (New York: Doubleday, 2010).

government, and many others." It's Anderson's opinion that, when push comes to shove, most Americans are more in line with core Catholic teachings.[2] I got a kick out of one survey released shortly before Christmas 2010. A Rasmussen Reports poll revealed that Christmas is a big holiday in the United States.[3] Stop the presses! Alert the authorities! By the surprised tone of the wire story, this was actually a pretty big story to members of the news media. The Rasmussen Reports Christmas survey showed that almost 90 percent of those who took part in the poll celebrate the holiday. And—you had better sit down for this one—despite the commercialization of the holiday season, the sacred component has not been lost. More than two-thirds of those who acknowledge Christmas say they consider it a "religious holiday".

We're not outnumbered. It's the other way around. Not that we run our lives by checking the latest poll results, but it sure is nice to know that we're in good company. This should encourage us to "be not afraid", as John Paul II reminded us so frequently, when it comes to defending our faith in the public square.

Pro-Life Efforts Are Having an Impact

"There are so many of them, and they are so young." Those are the revealing words of Nancy Keenan, the head of NARAL Pro-Choice America. Her comments came in a

---

[2] Carl Anderson, "Looking Past Extremes to Find America's Core Values", *Our Sunday Visitor Newsweekly* (January 23, 2011), http://www.osv.com/tabid/7621/itemid/7402/Looking-past-extremes-to-find-Americas-core-value.aspx.

[3] "Christmas Is the Number One Holiday Again This Year", December 24, 2010, http://www.rasmussenreports.com/public_content/lifestyle/holidays/december_2010/christmas_is_the_number_one_holiday_again_this_year.

Newsweek article following the 2010 March for Life in Washington, D.C. Keenan was traveling via train on the day of the march.

> When Keenan's train pulled into Washington's Union Station, a few blocks from the Capitol, she was greeted by a swarm of anti-abortion-rights activists. It was the 37th annual March for Life, organized every year on Jan. 22, the anniversary of Roe. "I just thought, my gosh, they are so young," Keenan recalled. "There are so many of them, and they are so young." [4]

Keenan's cause for concern is another reason for our hope. The pro-life movement is alive and well. It is also bursting with young people. I don't know if you have ever had the opportunity to attend the March for Life event in Washington, but if you do go, you will find that you come back encouraged, refreshed, and renewed. I actually call it the "shuffle for life"—there are so many people that we can't really march at all. We just sort of shuffle along with big smiles on our faces because we can see firsthand how the movement has grown and how it has a great future—because, as Keenan noted, so many young people are joining its ranks.

In an April 2010 interview with LifeSiteNews.com, the head of Students for Life of America explained how the fears of proabortion giants such as NARAL Pro-Choice America, Planned Parenthood, and the Feminist Majority are being played out at universities across the country as these abortion advocacy groups struggle to maintain student chapters of their organizations. "That's exactly what we see every day on college campuses. We'll have prochoice groups that spring up in reaction to the pro-life groups

---

[4] Sarah Kliff, "Remember Roe!", *Newsweek*, April 16, 2010, http://www.newsweek.com/2010/04/15/remember-roe.html.

that are started on campus and those groups, they maybe last a year. The only purpose they serve is to be reactionary towards our pro-life students." [5]

This is just one of the very visible ways in which we can witness how pro-life efforts are being felt—and why, I believe, we just may see an end to legalized abortion in our lifetime. The consistent grassroots education conducted by prolife groups since *Roe* has led to a major awakening of young Americans, who realize they are survivors of a holocaust. The growth of the pro-life youth movement is nothing short of astounding and is one of the brightest glimmers of hope on the horizon.

Catholic and Conservative Media Continue to Grow

In the mid- to late 1990s, there were only a handful of Catholic radio stations in the United States. Since then, the EWTN Global Catholic Radio Network has grown to include nearly 170 affiliates. Combine that number with other Catholic radio apostolates, and you will see some two hundred stations currently broadcasting Catholic programming. That doesn't include the outreach on satellite radio and the Internet, which allows Catholics to be heard around the world. I have personally received encouraging letters of support and gratitude from listeners in Great Britain, Ireland, and the Philippines, just to name a few. In the United States, EWTN radio affiliates have gone on the air in cities considered to be real mission fields for the faith, including San Francisco; Washington, D.C.; and Boston. This is just a small part of the evangelization explosion that is occurring

[5] Kathleen Gilbert, "NARAL's President Admits: Pro-Aborts Aging, Pro-Lifers Young and Zealous", April 21, 2010, http://www.lifesitenews.com/news/archive/ldn/2010/apr/10042108.

in the twenty-first century. The "spiritual beauty products" in your makeover goodie bag (see the end of chapter 7) are just a few samples of the Catholic outreach happening today. I could easily fill another book with the mile-long list of educational efforts under way in the Church.

And it is hard to deny the growth and the ratings of conservative media in America in the twenty-first century. The audiences for the major broadcast and cable networks continue to decline, while the ratings for radio and TV stations providing a voice for those with traditional values continue to increase.

Guess What? We Win in the End!

"And I tell you, you are Peter, and on this rock I will build my Church, and the gates of Hades shall not prevail against it" (Mt 16:18).

Jesus said that the Church will withstand all the attacks made against her, and if Jesus said so, that's good enough for me. It's actually pretty amazing when you think about it. The Catholic Church *has* to be the Church Christ founded; how else could she have survived all the attacks and scandals throughout the centuries and still be going strong two thousand years later?

Now, just because we know that the Lord and His Church will prevail, that doesn't mean that we can ignore suffering and injustice and go on living our merry little lives letting somebody else do all the hard work. By virtue of our Baptism, each one of us is called to evangelize. Whether we evangelize on the street corner, at the grocery store, in the home, or in the public square, we have a responsibility to tell our fellow man about salvation offered through Christ and the Catholic Church. Not every person has to march on his state capitol or run a worldwide ministry. But every

Christian has to do his part. I'll admit that there are days when "trying" is the last thing on my mind. I've lost track of how many times I have had the urge to shout that line from the old bubble bath commercial: "Calgon, take me away!" I get tired. I get frustrated. It seems that as soon as one fire is extinguished, another one starts burning out of control. That's when I recall the words of Blessed Teresa of Calcutta: "God has not called me to be successful; He has called me to be faithful." [6] It's uplifting now and again to see positive change taking place. It's a huge relief knowing that God is God and that we are not. The results are up to Him. Don't get discouraged. Be hopeful, and get busy doing God's work—beginning with yourself.

---

[6] Susan Conroy, *Mother Teresa's Lessons of Love and Secrets of Sanctity* (Huntington, Ind.: Our Sunday Visitor, 2003), p. 89.

Chapter 9

Let's Hear It for the Girls!

Testimonies Based on Timeless Truths

For with God nothing will be impossible.

—Luke 1:37

After reading my testimony book *Newsflash!*, a friend of mine, the pastor of a beautiful Byzantine Catholic Church in suburban Detroit, sent me a touching handwritten note reflecting how moved he was by reading the story of my journey back to the Catholic Church. He described my life as "a continuing series of miracles". I took that as a huge compliment meant not for me but for God. Considering my past life, the Lord really had His work cut out for Him when He took me on as a major work in progress.

My life is indeed a continuing series of miracles—so are the lives of the friends you're about to meet on the final pages of our extreme makeover journey. If I can change and they can change, anyone can change. While the names and the circumstances are different, the truths remain the same. Our hearts, as Saint Augustine reminds us, are restless until they rest in God, and no one, no matter how sinful or far away, is out of God's reach.

I Fled Him

Nina Brhyn, Dearborn, Michigan

> I fled Him, down the nights and down the days;
> I fled Him, down the arches of the years;
> I fled Him, down the labyrinthine ways
> Of my own mind; and in the mist of tears
> I hid from Him.
>
> —Francis Thompson, *The Hound of Heaven*

"Please take me to church, Mom!" I can still hear my daughter asking me over and over again to take her to church. As soon as she could speak, she would beg me to take her. I never went to church, nor did I speak of religion, faith, or Jesus or any other religious figure with any love or respect. I told my daughter that I did not believe in any of that "stuff", and I certainly did not believe that Jesus was the Son of God or my Savior. Why would I go to church, I said to her, if I didn't believe in any of what they told me there? She always replied: "Because I want to go, Mommy. Please come with me."

My daughter continued to ask me to go to church with her for several years. During this time, I was finishing my medical residency and eventually had my own practice. When we moved to a new town for work, I met many people who loved Jesus and offered to take my daughter to church with them. I let her go along, but I never went with her.

She was always very sad about my not joining her, and she would often ask me why I couldn't make her happy and go. As she got older, I often found myself thinking about her and her wish to go to church. Without knowing it, I was being drawn closer and closer to God through my child.

God, of course, works in mysterious ways. One day, a guest at our house told my daughter that her wish to say grace at the table was offensive to him. We never really said grace at our house, and my daughter had never insisted on saying it, but this day she did, and our guest was not appreciative. I saw my daughter's face crumble, and I knew she felt embarrassed and was worried she would be in trouble. At that moment, I broke all the rules of a good hostess, and I told this guest in so many words that if he had a problem with a little five-year-old saying grace, *he* could leave the table. I decided then and there that it was time for me to figure out for myself what and whom I believed in, if anything. I owed it to my children and myself to be able to look at them and articulate my own beliefs. If I were an atheist, so be it. If I were a Buddhist, that would be fine too. Of course, nowhere in my intellectually proud, pro-choice wildest dreams did I think I'd be a Catholic. I had no way of realizing that I was finally responding to the call God had been sending me all my life and that everything was about to change radically. I thought it was me looking for Him, but it was, of course, really Him looking for me.

Before I can tell you about the big changes that happened to me as I set out to discover my own faith, I have to take you back to show you how He had been "hounding" me for many, many years, wanting to pour His grace out on me. For Him to be able to fill me with that grace, I had to be ready to hear it, predisposed to receiving it, and willing to act on it when the moment and the right witness for me came along.

I was born in Norway in the mid-1960s, and I grew up in something close to utopia. I had a loving and well-off family, I went to good schools, I had friends, I traveled, and I went to school abroad. We had a summer house, a winter house, and a main residence, and we hobnobbed with all kinds of interesting and famous people. I was baptized into the Norwegian state church, but that was the only time in my life that I went to church with my parents outside of baptisms, weddings, or funerals. Organized religion was not a part of my life except for the time I was sent to a Catholic primary school. But I was sent there because it was a challenging and good school, not because my family believed in anything Catholics might believe in.

Norway at that time was a wonderful place for women in many ways. We had the world's first female prime minister, and the doors were wide open for women. I never had any sense of a glass ceiling or of barriers to anything I wanted to do. Child care was provided by the government, school was free all the way through university, and doctor and dentist visits were free until you reached the age of eighteen. Women were encouraged to take any job or receive any education they wanted. Abortion up until the twelfth week of pregnancy was legal and available on demand, and there was no expectation that women should stay "tied to the kitchen sink" with lots of kids and no career. We were told that we owned our own bodies and that we should enjoy the inherent sexuality of our bodies as well.

In reality, most of us figured out that sexuality was a lot more complex than we were being told and that getting pregnant and having an abortion was not something to want, or even to share with anyone. Having an abortion was painful and embarrassing, even in a society where it was discussed openly, where contraceptives were widely available, and where being sexually active was not even really frowned upon but rather expected. We even figured out that the birth control pill had many side effects that we found hard to live with, such as depression, weight gain, mood swings, and a lowered libido.

Despite this, I maintained the attitude my society had taught me—a staunch pro-choice, feminist attitude—all through my twenties and well into my thirties as I was finishing medical school and residency and even as I was having my own children.

Now, as I went out seeking a faith after my daughter's prompting had led me to want to clarify my beliefs, I did not even think that the Catholic Church was an option. I started by going to a local Zen Buddhist monastery and subsequently to a Tibetan Buddhist temple. I dropped by the local Quakers, the Bahá'is, and the Methodists, and I even read up on pagan beliefs. None of these religions did much for me, and I was beginning to think that my whole idea was silly and reactionary. I had lived a long time without a defined faith; why did I think I needed one now?

While I was going through all of this, I started to look back at my life. I could see that Christian people had constantly been put in my life ever since I was very young. There was the Pentecostal woman who rode the tram with me in the morning when I grew up in Oslo. She was always inviting me to come with her to "meet Jesus". There was one of my doctors when I was growing up, a charismatic who spoke in tongues incessantly and was always sending me tapes with Christian music. I finally wrote him a letter to tell him to stop and leave me alone. There were the nuns at the Gare du Nord, a Paris train station, who came up to me and told me that I was an angel from God and that I should listen for Him. I was on my way to catch a train to Venice, and I just kept on walking, gently rolling my eyes. There was my teacher in residency, Dr. Johnson, who one day looked at me and said: "Nina, it is not you looking for God, but Him looking for you!" He said this out of the blue while discussing leukemia, and I had no idea how to respond. Finally, there was, among too many others to mention, Dr. Jerry Brungardt, another one of my teachers in medical school and residency. A Catholic father of five children, he and his wife homeschooled and lived what appeared to be a very peaceful life. He never said a bad word about his wife, and she took care of the kids and the house and did the homeschooling. We, the residents, thought that the Brungardts were a little strange, and we certainly thought that five kids seemed like too many children for one couple to have. Imagine our shock when Jerry one day told us that his wife, for her birthday, asked for another baby! We pondered why they didn't think about the pill or other ways to avoid getting pregnant. When Jerry's wife, Cass, came to a Christmas party and told us that she and Jerry had once "contracepted" in their marriage and that it was a low point for both of them, we marveled not only at her candor but at the word *contracept*—we had never heard of a verb form of the word *contraception!* We had no idea how to respond, but the message did sink in and was stored in the back of my mind.

Throughout my residency, Jerry and Cass were very kind to me, and when I ended up as a divorced single mother, their love and support really carried me through some of the toughest days, days when I felt very alone. I still remember Jerry telling me they had prayed a Rosary for me as a family. I had no idea what that meant, and I was a little taken aback, but I did recognize that they were expressing love for me.

So, as I was setting out to find my faith, I was thinking back to all these people who had clearly been "hounding me" to tell me that God loved me, but it was always in the context of a Christian God. I wasn't sure what that meant for me. My pro-choice attitude and the fact that I had many wonderful gay friends were two of the main reasons I did not like the Catholic Church and why even Christianity in general seemed uninviting to me. I thought that the Church was hateful to both women and homosexuals, and I didn't see how her attitude toward them could be considered merciful and loving. Of course, it also seemed silly to me that God would have to sacrifice His Son for us. How pagan of an image, I remember thinking, that the Creator of all would need a blood sacrifice!

At this time, I was moving from one city to another, and I wanted to homeschool my children. I sent off letters to several groups in the city I was moving to at the time, but only one responded back. Cathy M. was the leader of the local Catholic homeschool group, and she sent me a package to introduce herself and the group. Since I wasn't Catholic, I thought it was a little funny that she was the only one to respond, but I read all the materials and called the contact number I was given. The woman at the other end was very nice but became a little reserved when she realized I was not a Catholic. Her name was Linda, and she was kind enough to invite me into her home. My children, who didn't know anyone in the area because we had just moved there, suddenly had a family of six kids to play with. Linda was never pushy or unkind, but she also never compromised her beliefs. When she and her husband found out that my partner and I were not married, they told us that their kids would not be allowed to come to our house but that we were welcome to come to theirs anytime. I went there often, enjoying both their food and their company, and Linda and I had many discussions about faith, love, hope, and all the other things that mattered to both of us.

One day about four months after the move, I was driving around town, getting ready to give a talk to some medical students. In the packet that Cathy M. had sent me about the homeschoolers, there was a CD by a professor of moral theology, Janet Smith, Ph.D. I had no idea who this person was, and the title of the CD seemed to be designed just to make me laugh. "Contraception: Why Not?" sounded to me, a pro-choice physician, like something made up by medical students to make fun of their faculty. But for some reason, I decided to pop the CD in my CD player and listen to it as I drove the forty minutes to the hospital for my talk. For those of you who aren't familiar with Smith's presentation, in it she goes through a wonderful and witty—but also sharp and intellectually honest—assessment of why contraception harms marriage. She ties everything into the papal encyclical *Humanae Vitae* by Pope Paul VI and its insistence that contraception is not acceptable to faithful Catholics.

Now, I had always been intellectually proud, and one of the things I could always count on in my pride was that my adversaries never read or studied as much as I did. I could always cite books, documents, and other sources to back up my point, and people did not like debating with me because I was argumentative and somewhat of a bully. All of this stemmed, of course, from pride.

Well, I had in previous times argued against *Humanae Vitae*. I had shrieked and sighed that an unmarried, chaste man in Rome could hardly know anything about my situation as a woman, married, sexually active, and far removed in time and space from the Catholic Church's draconian vision of marriage and the sexes. But as I listened to Smith's talk, I realized that I had never read *Humanae Vitae*. The Achilles heel of all my opponents was now mine. I had no idea that the Holy Father had said that the use of contraception would make it easier for men to objectify women, that men would stop caring about women's physical and psychological welfare and just use them for pleasure. I had no idea that he predicted that women would start to treat their bodies as machines and that childbearing would become nothing more than another "thing" their bodies could do, commercialized and industrialized.

As I listened to that talk, I had a moment like Paul on the way to Damascus. When I got into the car to start driving, I was pro-choice, procontraception, not Catholic, and definitely not a friend of Pope Paul VI. But at a certain moment during this talk, I felt the sun blind me, and tears started to stream down my face. How could I not have seen the incredible beauty in the Catholic Church; the veracity of her teachings; the true love of God, constantly showing itself to me through so many people, and now through the explanation of *Humanae Vitae* by Janet Smith? My hubris was clear to me, and the truth—as in *the* Truth, with a capital *T*—hit me like the proverbial ton of bricks. I understood that I had, through my own fault, been intellectually dishonest in discussing *Humanae Vitae* and, by extension, probably many other Church teachings that I had assumed I knew but now saw that I did not know. I remembered Cass saying that contraception had been bad for her and her husband in their marriage. I remembered how even we as teenagers and young adults back in liberal and lovely Norway had recognized that contraception and abortions were bad for us as women. I remembered thinking that I thought abortion was acceptable. But how could I think the industrialized slaughter of innocent humans was right? I thought of Linda's endless generosity with me and my kids, feeding us and offering us a friendship when we were brand-new in town, even though I was not a Catholic, was not married, was living with my boyfriend, and had no qualms about it! I remembered all the other people who had tried to show me that God was looking for me. I could see my little daughter begging me to go to church with her—and everything came together in one beautiful, sunny day in my car. I realized right then that I had to reevaluate everything I had ever believed and that I had to get to a Catholic Church as soon as I could.

The epilogue to this story is simple. Linda sent me to a wonderful and orthodox priest who took in me and my now husband and children for RCIA, Rite of Christian Initiation of Adults. We were all confirmed in the Catholic Church at the 2006 Easter Vigil. My husband and I have a fourth child, and every day, we see more and more what great things God has done for us and continues to do. He is always looking for all of us, He invites us to have a relationship with Him, and He loves us all beyond measure. I will thank Him endlessly for never giving up on me, a sinner, and for allowing me to see and feel His love, His mercy, His outpouring of grace onto me. He called me by name. I hope you hear Him calling for you too.

> Ah, fondest, blindest, weakest,
> I am He Whom thou seekest!
> Thou drawest love from thee, who drawest Me.
>
> —Francis Thompson, *The Hound of Heaven*

From Revert to Pro-Life Activist

Janet Morana, Executive Director of Priests for Life, Metuchen, New Jersey

I was born in Brooklyn, New York, in 1952 and was educated in Catholic schools. I am the oldest of four children, with fourteen years separating me from my youngest sibling. I grew up before the Second Vatican Council, so the Catholic Church and liturgy were very different from what they are today. The Mass was all in Latin, the altar was against the wall, and the priest celebrated Mass with his back to the congregation. This was called the Tridentine Mass. Women had to have their heads covered with either a hat or a chapel veil before entering the church. You genuflected before entering the pew, and the tabernacle was at the front and center of the church—not like in some churches today, where you have to go on a search-and-find mission to locate Jesus in the tabernacle! Our catechesis was from the Baltimore Catechism, which was in a question-and-answer format.

Spiritual direction was something that just didn't exist for the average layperson. You memorized all your prayers, and you had your Saint Joseph Missal to follow the Mass. Just about every Saturday afternoon, you would come in from playing to change your clothes and walk over to church for Confession. Sunday morning, you lined up in the school yard for the 9:00 A.M. children's Mass. Church was a place of warmth, comfort, and stability. In fact, when meeting new people, you commonly identified yourself by the name of your parish—mine was Saint Vincent Ferrer, in the

177

Flatbush section of Brooklyn, New York. But you would just say, "I'm from Saint Vinny's!"

Then came 1965, the end of the Second Vatican Council, and the Church of my childhood was about to undergo some radical changes. The whole look of "Saint Vinny's" began to change: the altar was turned around, the priest faced the congregation, and the Mass was now all in English. Latin hymns and organ music practically vanished, and in came guitars, tambourines, and folk music. The tabernacle was dismissed to a side altar, the beautiful marble altar railing was removed, and we no longer knelt to receive Communion; in fact, we were encouraged to receive Jesus in our hands rather than on our tongues, which was unthinkable before the Council. Confession could now take place face-to-face with the priest, although this same priest began to discourage weekly Confession anyway—a monthly or even a "seasonal" confession was considered fine. Women no longer had to have their heads covered upon entering church; genuflecting almost became passé. What happened to that feeling that when you entered the church, you were in awe at being in the presence of the Almighty, the one true God? Now it was like we were high-fiving Jesus! Imagine being an adolescent going through this—the one sure, stable thing that you thought you could count on was radically changing. This was a time that tried people's souls.

I was attending a small, all-girl Catholic high school at the time, Saint Agnes Seminary in Brooklyn, staffed by the Sisters of Saint Joseph. In my sophomore year, the Church went through another radical change. July 25, 1968, is a day that will live in Church infamy—the date that Pope Paul VI issued *Humanae Vitae*. There was division in the Church. You could literally go to a priest on one side of a church and be told that using contraception was a sin, while on the other side of the same church another priest would say it wasn't a sin as long as you had a "good reason" to use it. Let's face it—we can all try and justify our behavior if we really want to.

The culture too was changing. In came the sexual revolution, the "women's lib" movement, and the drug culture. And I too got caught up in this whole changing world. I began to question my faith. I thought women had a right to use contraception, and I no longer believed in the infallibility of the Pope. All those Baltimore Catechism questions and answers became irrelevant to me.

Then the moment came when I took that first step down the slippery slope. It was my sophomore year, and the priest came to our school for our monthly Confession. I dutifully lined up with my class for Confession. This time, though, I began to feel anxious and no longer wanted to go to Confession. I did an about-face and walked back into class. Sister said, "Confession, Janet!" and I replied, "Yes, Sister", and this lie began my first step down that slippery slope. I stopped going to Confession, which led me to abstain from Communion, which in turn led to me skipping Mass altogether. In the end, I attended Mass only on Christmas and Easter.

Fast-forward a little. I graduated from Saint Francis College in 1974 and married in 1975. It was a time when my Catholic faith no longer seemed to matter to me. My relationship with God was almost at a zero. At that time, all my close friends were getting married, so marriage seemed like the next step to take—or so I thought.

I became engaged after dating my future husband for three months. From there, things moved quickly toward our wedding day. At Pre-Cana classes, the priest told us that depending upon the circumstances, birth control pills could be an option for us to consider. I didn't realize at the time that this was bad advice in every way: theologically, spiritually, psychologically, and physically.

As the oldest of four siblings, I had many years of experience dealing with diapers and baby-sitting and felt that delaying the start of a family was a good idea. I had taken birth control pills back in high school (although I wasn't sexually active), as prescribed by my Catholic gynecologist for menstrual problems. At this point in my life, then, both a priest and a doctor had legitimized the use of contraceptives, and so I continued my journey down the slippery slope.

I started taking birth control pills three months before my wedding day. About one month before the wedding, my fiancé began to pressure me to have sex with him. I had been a virgin up until then. I gave in to the pressure, and so my marriage got off to a bad start. When you begin marriage not knowing each other very well and then compound things by moving into a very intimate physical relationship, you set the stage for disaster. There's a popular song about marrying your best friend; well, that's how well you should know someone before entering into such a serious, lifelong commitment.

I continued taking the pill for two years. Once I was off the pill, I got pregnant immediately and gave birth to an absolutely beautiful baby girl. I threw all my attention into motherhood and as a result wanted to delay having another baby. I went back on birth control pills until my daughter was thirteen months old. I then felt it was important for her to have a sibling, so I stopped taking the pill. Once again, I became pregnant almost immediately. The lesson I was teaching myself was this: No pill equals countless children!

This time I gave birth to beautiful twin girls. By this time, information was released showing that a higher risk of blood clots and strokes was associated with taking birth control pills. With a history of strokes in my family, I was afraid to go back on the pill. I didn't know about Natural Family Planning. In fact, the only natural method that I knew of was the old "rhythm" method, which was considered by most to be unreliable. Since my marriage was built on a physical relationship, you can imagine the amount of arguing and fighting that began. When the twins were three, I thought I was pregnant again. It was just a scare, but it was enough to make me do something really drastic: I had a tubal ligation. I felt I had solved all my problems—or so I thought.

I had embraced everything that the feminist movement promoted as being liberating and empowering for women. But in reality, I had not been liberated; every day, I felt more trapped in a bad marriage.

As my marriage continued its downward spiral, I focused more and more on my three daughters. The good news is that I became reconnected with my Catholic faith around this time. It was amazing how the hand of God worked. You see, I was trying to get a job teaching in the public schools in Staten Island, but they weren't hiring; there were, in fact, budget cuts. My mother-in-law, who was a daily communicant and also the person who took my daughters to Mass every Sunday for me, began praying a novena that I would find a job. I just rolled my eyes, being the doubting Thomasina that I was. It was two days before Christmas 1988 that I was hired to teach first grade in P.S. 31 in Staten Island. It was a miracle! My mother-in-law instructed me to go to Church to light a candle of thanksgiving.

Well, since it was Christmas and I at least went to Mass then, I went and lit my candle. I then also went to Mass the following Sunday, not wanting to chance anything happening to my starting my new teaching position. By my third week of attending Mass, the hand of God reached out for me again. We were leaving church when my daughter Tara Lynn called out to the newly ordained Father Frank Pavone to come over and meet her mom. She said, "Father

Frank, here's my mom—you know, the one that needs to go to Confession!" I turned beet red with embarrassment. Father Pavone was very cool and calmed down Tara Lynn's excitement and turned to me and told me I didn't have to go to Confession. Well, that was a relief. He did give me the rectory phone number and told me to give him a call. He said we could just talk. Just talk about the Church? That seemed odd to me. So I stuffed the paper with his number in my pocketbook, and there it stayed for a few more weeks. Then one day I stumbled across it again and decided to give this young priest a call. He invited me to his Friday night Bible class, and we had an appointment for what I later found out was called spiritual direction after that. I gave him my laundry list of disagreements with the Church's teaching, and he wasn't shocked. He invited me to continue to come and study, and I took him up on the challenge. It took me three months of discussion and study, and finally I was ready for Confession. After twenty years away from the Church, I rediscovered the wealth we have with our faith. I received Communion that day, and it was like my First Holy Communion. I know this was beginning a relationship with Jesus.

As I continued to rediscover my faith and the teachings of the Church, I learned about God's beautiful plan for marriage, including Natural Family Planning.

At the same time, I became aware of how birth control pills really worked.

I had always thought that birth control pills simply prevented fertilization. But now I learned that the pill actually has its own built-in insurance system, employing several different methods of action in case one or more of the methods don't work. Besides trying to prevent fertilization by suppressing ovulation, the pill also thickens the cervical mucus, which then acts as a barrier, preventing sperm from getting to the egg. If both of these first two methods fail and ovulation and conception both occur, then the pill acts to prevent the fertilized egg (the newly conceived human being) from implanting itself into the wall of the uterus. The child is then aborted, flushed out of the body.

I didn't feel the impact of this newfound information until several years later. I was with a friend visiting the Epcot Center in Disney World, and we decided to visit the Wonders of Life exhibit. As I began to watch a beautiful video showing the wonder of how human life begins, I realized what my taking birth control pills really meant: the possibility that I had aborted new life. In the years that I had been taking birth control pills, I had been very sexually active. I also knew that I was an extremely fertile woman. Given these facts, there is no doubt that I had successfully conceived new life many times but had never given these little babies the chance to grow inside me. For the very first time in my life, I came to grips with the fact that I had not only shut myself off to life but had also destroyed an unknown number of children.

As I came out of that exhibit, there was a giant rushing water fountain nearby. I walked over to it and began to sob uncontrollably. I stayed there for quite some time, absorbed in my sudden feelings of grief and remorse. This was the very first time I became aware of the full impact of what I had done.

As I became more involved in pro-life work, I learned more about the damage that abortion does to women. I realized that many women who had had abortions had felt alone in their grief at first but later were able to experience mercy and healing. These women who had been through the healing process could therefore serve as a voice for other women still locked in the secret sin of abortion. That is why I cofounded the Silent No More Awareness Campaign,

an initiative that gives women a forum for publicly testify-
ing to the negative impact that abortion had on their lives.
Because I had never had a surgical abortion, people began
to question why I was involved in such a campaign. Here
again I had to come to grips with all the children I had lost
because of birth control pills.

Most people who work in postabortion ministry recognize only the pain and grief from surgical abortion. Yet I
know in my heart that the loss I feel is just as real as if I had
had a surgical abortion. Moreover, I know I am not alone.
In fact, many women come up to me when I am at conferences speaking about the Silent No More Awareness Campaign and share their grief from years of taking abortifacients.

But there is good news. I was able to come to grips with
these feelings of grief and loss recently at a Rachel's Vine-
yard retreat. It was a first step in having my feelings vali-
dated, and I began to deal with my loss in a new light. I
am here to say that I will be "silent no more" about the
children that I aborted through contraception.

I am now reaching out to the other women who I know
share these feelings. I am sure I am not the only woman
with a testimony like this. I want others that would like to
share their story to send it to me. I have established a section on the Priests for Life website for these testimonies. I
know that by getting the word out, we can help many families realize the damage contraception will do to their lives.
I also want to reach out to others who feel the pain that I
have described and tell them that they too can take the first
steps toward healing.

Finally, it is my hope that others like me who turned
their back on Jesus and the Church will realize the true
wealth we have in the documents and teachings of the
Church. Our purpose in life is, as the Baltimore Catechism
said, "to know Him, to love Him, and to serve Him in this

world, and to be happy with Him forever in the next". Ah, but we are also called to know Jesus Christ as our Lord and Savior and also as our Friend. We are called to have a personal relationship with Him. I nearly threw this all away; I was away from Him for almost twenty years. I will spend whatever time I have left here on earth singing His praises and hopefully through my story bring others back to the Lord and His bride, the Church!

He Forgives You

Mary Lockwood, Plymouth, Michigan

My name is Mary, and my husband is John. We are very ordinary and are probably a lot like many other couples you know—couples who might have an abortion in their past. But we are special by virtue of the fact that we know and understand, in spite of our sins of abortion, that God loves us, and loves us unconditionally. That makes us special— you are all special.

Let me share a little of my journey of forgiveness and healing. I might be like someone you know; I might be a little like you; I might be like someone in your own family, or one of your friends, or a neighbor; or I might be like someone sitting next to you in the church pew. I might be like someone you know who has had all the right upbringing but still made very bad decisions—decisions I will regret and feel remorseful about for the rest of my life. People like me and you make wrong decisions every day, for we know not what we do.

This story is not so much about me, or John, or us as a couple, but is more about God's love and mercy and forgiveness. The words I speak when I tell my story in front of others are not my public confession but rather the sharing of what God's unconditional love has done for me personally. I was invited by a friend and confessor to speak out; I am inviting you to know the forgiveness and healing our Lord has for you, or for someone you might know who made wrong decisions as I did. I can't say it enough: *He loves us all unconditionally.*

What I am about to tell you is not something I am proud of. Unfortunately, there is absolutely nothing I can do about what I did except to go forth and do some good with it and to share my story with as many people as I possibly can.

Just for a moment, let me take you back to the 1970s, when abortion was first made legal. You might have thought of abortions as something that happened in secretive places or in dirty, dark surroundings—and they did—but the truth about my abortions is that they were all paid for by my group health care plan. My abortions were performed in a Detroit hospital, a very sterile setting, by competent doctors, doctors with their own families at home. I was given no counseling whatsoever, and no questions were asked. The procedure was surgically clean, it was discreet, and there was no aftermath.

No aftermath? So I thought. I thought it was my body, my choice. Without regard to God as the giver of life, without regard to the sin of abortion, I had only me to think about. Again, so I thought. I did not understand, fully, that my body was created by God and is a gift. I didn't respect my body, or the life within me.

I have had multiple abortions. Two of them were when I got pregnant by "just another guy", a guy who meant nothing, and one was when I got pregnant by my future husband (we weren't married at the time). You might ask, and I am sure it is a question in your mind as you read this about this Catholic girl, "Why three abortions?" You might ask also, "Didn't she learn the first time?" "Didn't she understand what she did was wrong?" I was very confused and didn't understand much between right and wrong when I was faced with these unwanted pregnancies. There wasn't much right with my life at that point. I treated abortion as a birth control method, one that worked a lot better than the oral contraceptives that failed me. How twisted my thinking was then. I was emotionally and spiritually deficient and did not understand my faith or my God. The third abortion, in 1987, was the one involving my now husband. He was in New York, and I was in Michigan, feeling totally alone and afraid to face pregnancy. He had a great job in New York, and I had my corporate career. We never deeply talked about our abortion until we started publicly speaking together as a postabortive couple. It has been a painful—and I mean painful—journey, yet it has also been revealing and rewarding. It has been a journey filled with God's forgiveness and healing. God has forgiven me and has wiped the slate clean. Great sin is the occasion for great grace.

I stayed away from the Church because I felt so ashamed of myself and felt so sinful. I did not think I could be forgiven for what I had done because I did not understand God's love and therefore His forgiveness. I started going to Mass again every once in a while and by choice, or so I thought, one Sunday I went to a different Mass at a local retreat center in suburban Detroit. I definitely was called there because the homily that Sunday was all about God's unconditional love for each and every one of us, and how He forgives sin, no matter what. It was as if God was pulling me in—and did He ever.

For years, I did not accept God's forgiveness and unconditional love. I had denied and minimized what God had done for me. He died on the Cross for my sins, for the sins of all of us. God's forgiveness—and my forgiveness of myself and of those men in my life—have given me my life back.

I thought no one would be hurt by my decision. The truth is, each and every abortion hurts each and every one of us.

It destroys life. I am now using my horrible decision of abortion to fight for those who cannot fight for themselves. Imagine if your mother had considered an abortion. Perhaps you say to yourself, "Oh, that would never have happened!" But I made that decision. Young women and men make that decision each day—no one knows how a particular person will react in that situation. Again, each and every abortion hurts each and every one of us—our families, our daughters, our wives, our sisters, our husbands, our boyfriends, our sons, our brothers, our society.

What I would like to leave you with is the knowledge that in spite of our sin, in spite of our past, God is all-merciful and forgiving—if you come to Him with a repentant heart. Your past does *not* define you. God loves us all unconditionally. Go to Him, and His love and forgiveness and mercy will give you new life.

Yes, Lord!

Kathy Crombie, Dearborn, Michigan

For a good portion of my adult life, I had issues—issues with the Roman Catholic Church, that is. Interestingly, though, I did not plan to leave my Catholic faith anytime soon; I just wanted to fix it. I had issues with the fact that women were not allowed to be priests; that praying through Mary seemed ridiculous when we could go right to Jesus; that the Rosary was a useless and repetitious prayer; that to receive forgiveness for sins, Catholics had to tell their sins to a man, the priest; that the Pope was infallible; and that contraception and abortion were considered evil by the Catholic Church when just about everyone else embraced them.

After Robyn and I were married in 1972, we soon found out I could no longer take the birth control pill due to medical complications. This was a huge problem for us because we had decided we did not want children. Our lives were about "us" and what we wanted to do and when we wanted to do it. We didn't see this as selfish but rather as sticking to our plan for success and happiness. Children, we thought, would change our lives forever and not allow us the freedom we deserved. For us, contraception was the answer. Regarding abortion, I knew that I could never have one myself, but I fully believed I had no right to tell another woman what to do with her body—her body, her choice. After much thought and discussion with my husband, we decided that I would get an IUD (intrauterine device).

An IUD is a small object inserted through the cervix of a woman and placed in the uterus to prevent pregnancy. I was told that the IUD needed to be checked for positioning in a couple of months and that it needed to be removed after three years. That's it. After several months, I learned I was pregnant. Robyn and I were not happy with the news. My doctor immediately told me that I needed to make a decision about the IUD—leave it in or take it out. He said that if I left it in, the IUD would probably do what it was designed to do, and I'd have a miscarriage; if I took it out, there would be less of a chance of this occurring. I soon came to the understanding that this life inside of me was a child—although this was not my first thought—and I could not willingly jeopardize the life of my baby. I instructed the doctor to take the IUD out. Nine months later our first son, Derek, was born, a beautiful and healthy baby boy.

I realize now, all these years later, that even though the doctor never used the word *abortion*, IUDs are abortifacients. That means they are designed to abort a pregnancy if one occurs. The IUD inflames the uterine lining, making it impossible for a newly conceived human being to implant into the wall of the uterus. That IUD was like a little abortion machine inside of me, standing at the ready to destroy all innocent human life at its earliest stages. My husband and I were set up for automatic abortions as often as a pregnancy might occur. Lord, have mercy, as that was never our intention.

To be honest, my husband and I have no idea how many little abortions took place within me during our use of the IUD. It could have been zero, although that is doubtful. We'll never really know. What we know now is that the IUD is considered one of the most effective forms of birth control on the market today. Notice that I said *birth control* and not *contraceptive*. Although in our society these two terms are often misunderstood to mean the same thing, they do not. Contraception blocks conception. Birth control can include contraception and more—namely, abortion. In time, God blessed us with another son, Chad. When he graduated from high school, he was diagnosed with Hodgkin's disease—a nonlymphomatous cancer. My husband and I were devastated. Chad's medical team planned out a course of radiation treatment. It was at the same time that God allowed His mercy and His healing hand to bless us. Through a very close friend, Chad and I were introduced to a man named Irving "Francis" Houle. My friend said, "We need to get Chad to Francis. I expect nothing less than a miracle." Francis received the wounds of Christ in his hands when Jesus appeared to him in 1993. Jesus told him, "I'm taking away your hands and giving you Mine—touch My children." When Chad prayed with Francis, and Francis laid the wounded hands of Christ on my son, he was miraculously healed. When I prayed with Francis, and he laid the wounded hands of Christ on me, God sent a walloping dose of the Holy Spirit that changed my life—and the lives of many people whom God now places in my path. Recently I learned that this experience is called being baptized in the Spirit, when the third Person of the Blessed Trinity descends upon you and provides the gifts you need to do God's work. To this day, fifteen years later, Chad remains healed, and I am on fire for my Catholic faith.

God tackled the issues I had with the Catholic Church, one by one. I learned that women could not become priests because Jesus calls only men to the priesthood—and not every man is called. It's a vocation and not a job. I learned that the fastest way to get to Jesus is when we hold the hand of His Blessed Mother; she is the road map to Jesus. I learned that the priest is the man I see in the confessional, but it's Jesus the High Priest who forgives my sins when the priest speaks the words of absolution. I learned that the Pope is the Vicar of Christ in apostolic succession. And I learned that contraception and abortion are always, always, always wrong because they do not promote the dignity and sanctity of human life—life created by God in His image and likeness. Soon after my conversion, He called me to the pro-life movement as a volunteer, and even though it scared me to death, I sheepishly obeyed and followed Him.

Several years after my conversion, I discerned that God was preparing me for a job change. I had a pretty clear interior sense that something was coming—I just didn't understand why it was taking so long or what it would be, so I continued to pray to know His will and direction. In retrospect, I can see He was softening my heart to accept His will—to move from working full time in the world of visual arts to working full time in the pro-life movement.

I left my development position at a prestigious art museum to become the director of gift planning for a very prominent and successful pro-life organization. And on top of this, God also called me to leave my work as an artist at the same time. I had created signature, one-of-a-kind contemporary baskets using natural materials; I pushed the definition of a basket to its very limits to create lyrical, nonfunctional vessels that sold in galleries and to private collectors. I worked hard to achieve all this, and now God was asking me to give all that up too? In the end, although it was a difficult decision, that's what I did, and I never looked back.

After I had made my decision, I read Pope John Paul II's Letter to Artists.[1] This little document touched me deeply.

---

[1] "Letter of His Holiness Pope John Paul II to Artists" (April 4, 1999), Holy See website, http://www.vatican.va/holy_father/john_paul_ii/letters/documents/hf_jp-ii_let_23041999_artists_en.html.

Here was a man, the Pope no less, who understood my
heart as an artist. It wasn't long after that that I felt God
calling me back to the arts. I felt as if He was saying to me,
"I did not give you all that talent to do nothing with it—use
it for My glory." So I prayed again, trying to understand
His plan for me.

Sometimes, God lets me know what He wants, and I
clearly understand right away; at other times, I sense He's
asking something of me, but I'm not quite sure what it is.
In those latter instances, my prayer has become, "If this is
not of You, Lord, slam the door shut." I used this latter
prayer when the Lord asked me to go back to the arts,
because I did not know what exactly it was that He wanted
me to do. I just put one foot in front of the other and
stepped out in faith; it took years before I understood.

To make a very long story short, a friend told me about
a school of sacred art one day. She advised me to check it
out. The only workshop that fit my schedule was a week-
long course on iconography. What did I know about icons?
I knew that the word *icon* meant image. I knew that they
looked kind of weird and distorted. I knew that they were
pictures of Jesus, Mary, the angels, and the saints and were
considered very holy, but that's it. Committing all this to
prayer, I decided to step out in faith and take the course. I
rediscovered my artistic talents and how they could be used
for God and not just my own success.

God has blessed my Yes both to the pro-life movement
and to my work as an iconographer. Both are about the
sacredness of the human person, who is created in the image
and likeness of God. When it was all happening, I did not
see this thread of His image in my pro-life work and iconography, but it's all very clear now.

What's also very clear is that my work as a basket artist
was never about Him; it was about what I wanted to achieve

as an artist. Iconography is very different. As an iconographer, you don't sign the completed work because it's not yours. God is the Divine Artist. Every work session begins and ends in prayer. An iconographer continues to pray and humbly submits his will to God's as he mixes the paint and holds the brush for the Lord. There's something quite beautiful about all of this. And believe me, I have no grand illusion that I am a gifted iconographer; it's all the Lord, and I can't take any credit for what He has allowed me to do.

I'm going on my eleventh year as a pro-life professional, and my sixth year as an iconographer. To date, I've written eleven icons, of which three have been permanently or temporarily installed for public veneration: one in a church, one in a chapel, and one in a cathedral. On the feast of Our Lady of Sorrows on September 15, 2010, one of these icons, the life-size *Icon of Jesus, the Divine Mercy*, was blessed for public veneration for the Servants of Jesus of the Divine Mercy and for the Divine Mercy Center in Eastpointe, Michigan. The icon has been installed in the chapel of the Divine Mercy Center. God is clearly working through this icon to touch many, many people and draw them to His unfathomable mercy. The point I wish to share with you is this: it is illogical that on my own I would have been able to write such impressively beautiful icons after taking only one course. That is how I know that God is ultimately the artist. I can certainly take credit for my Yes to Him, but that's about it. To God be all the praise and glory.

Looking back on my life, I see now that God's plan all along was to bless me and my husband through our children. It seems very simple now. My husband and I were very selfish in initially deciding we did not want a family. What were we thinking? Our lives are full today because God mercifully rejected our plan, despite all our attempts, and implemented His own. As a result, we have two wonderful sons, a beautiful daughter-in-law, and two loving grandchildren. Through them all, Robyn and I see God's love and mercy, and we did nothing to deserve it. In a particular way, I am reminded every day that I am here to serve Him through all those created in His image and likeness. I am blessed to do so through all those God places in my path, through my family, and in the iconography He has called me to do for His glory. All He asks for is our Yes.

Yours for Life

Astrid Bennett Gutierrez, Executive Director of Los Angeles Pregnancy Services (LAPS), Los Angeles, California

My parents were in their early twenties when they met and married in Los Angeles, California. My mother was an immigrant raised in the small town of Tepechtitlan in Zacatecas, Mexico, in a large, traditional Catholic family. My father was raised in El Salvador, though he was born in Los Angeles of an Irish American father and a Salvadoran mother who had been an exchange student in America. Catholicism was mostly cultural for my parents. However, they both shared a fascination for history, literature, and the arts. (These interests had the happy effect of communicating a sense of beauty and nobility to my heart, making it a more fertile ground for faith.) In fact, it was my mother's curiosity about Communism that led her to spend time with a Cuban lady who would introduce her to my father. I was born in 1973, a year after they were married, thanks to my mom having rejected an offer of money for birth control pills by a family friend. I imagine that my mom reacted from an instinctive sense of modesty and morality at this bold, misguided recommendation. The knowledge of my mom's righteous action would later help to inspire me to fight against the evil of contraception.

Despite their many struggles and limitations, my parents were loving and dedicated to my sister, Diana, and me. I believe that this sense of closeness, particularly with my dad, and the certainty that I was loved by him prepared my heart to better

understand the unconditional love of God the Father. Though
my parents were not very devout, they did try to follow important religious traditions. They baptized me at the age of three
during a trip to El Salvador; I walked right up to the baptis-
mal font! To ensure that Diana and I would receive a good
academic education, my parents sacrificed greatly to send us
to parochial school. My father worked as the school's janitor
part time to help pay the tuition. The kindness of the Clar-
etian Missionary sisters who taught us left an indelible mem-
ory of what spiritual motherhood truly meant.

When I was eight years old, my parents' marriage began
to fall apart from economic pressures and from poor advice
from family and friends. I remember wishing that my parents were more spiritual, that they would pray that wonderful prayer that the sister taught us about, the Rosary.
She instructed us, "If you pray one Mystery as a family, it
is great, and if you pray the entire Rosary, that would be
wonderful!" I brought home a bumper sticker that she gave
us that had the famous quote from Father Patrick Peyton,
"The family that prays together stays together", which I
pasted on the headboard of my bed like a last desperate cry.

My parents eventually separated. Even though my father
lived apart from us after the separation, he still spent time
with my sister and me. Concerned by the current affairs of
our day, especially the Cold War during the eighties, he
hoped we would one day become diplomats. At the age of
ten, I began to learn Russian with my father. A love for
languages and a concern for the world beyond my doorstep
began then. That same year, Father moved out of state and
then out of the country, leaving a huge void in my heart.
My mother's emotional unavailability because of the tre-
mendous amount of pressure and stress she had as a single
parent also left me feeling alone and depressed. Only God
could fill this void—blessed, happy void!

I was confirmed at age thirteen by the late Bishop Carl Fisher, a courageous advocate of the unborn. During his homily, he walked up to my pew and asked me point blank: "If someone asked you if you believed in God, and if you answered yes they would shoot you, what would you say?" My answer to him was, "I would say yes." Several of the people in the congregation found my response amusing and laughed. The bishop smiled and said, "Most people would answer that they would find that situation difficult. But you would say yes? I will never forget you." My answer surprised him, but it flowed from the inspiration I felt from reading the stories of saints and admiring their example. My confirmation saint was Maria Goretti, a young martyr. The desire to give my life heroically to God would remain in my heart.

In Catholic high school, I continued to embrace a faith in God, but I became more relativistic about it as I imbibed the work of dismal secular thinkers, such as the existentialist Jean-Paul Sartre. I remember no mention of any of the great Catholic philosophers, such as Gabriel Marcel, Dietrich von Hildebrand, and Edith Stein. Sorely missing from my Catholic education as well was a strong sense of the supernatural and of reverence, the most fundamental of virtues. In addition, the lack of a fervent life of faith at home and proper instruction from the pulpit (when my class actually bothered to go to Mass) made me ill prepared to face the world. My morals would be severely challenged at the famously liberal University of California, Berkeley. It was there that I first seriously questioned the Catholic faith of my childhood. I wrote a paper for my English class where I denounced the Church's position on homosexuality. So misinformed was I on the profoundly beautiful and essential teachings of the Church on man, woman, and marriage that I had very little with which to defend myself against the aggressive culture of death and moral relativism that surrounded me. Not being able to withstand the costs (morally as well as financially), I returned home for good after one year at Berkeley and attended UCLA. My faith had been severely tested, and I had not fared very well. Shaken by this year at Berkeley, I became lukewarm and disheartened about my faith.

At the age of twenty-one, I was blessed with a beautiful relationship with a young Protestant man. God used that time to enable me to recover and deepen my sense of family, marriage, and faith. Cultural and religious differences that were really not very important to us became excuses to argue—we were under severe stress from school and were not very mature emotionally—and the relationship fell apart. I realized how little I knew about the Catholic faith that I tried to defend. I enrolled at UCLA, the University of California at Los Angeles, to finish my bachelor's degree shortly after this breakup. I had been left feeling sad, as if I was spiritually lost once again.

During my first quarter at UCLA, I saw an announcement in the university newspaper, the *Daily Bruin*, for a meeting of the John Paul II Society, a group run by graduate students who were members of Opus Dei.[1] The very first meeting was led by a convert to the Catholic faith from the Mormon church. He told a heart-wrenching story of the sacrifices he had to make to follow Christ and the true Church. This was the first time that I had met a convert to the Catholic faith. (I did not even know that they existed; I had witnessed only the exodus of poorly catechized Latino Catholics to Protestant churches.) He also shared the stories of nineteenth-century Catholic intellectuals, such as John Henry Cardinal Newman, G. K. Chesterton, and

---

[1] Opus Dei is a Catholic institution founded by Saint Josemaria Escrivá. Its mission is to spread the message that work and the circumstances of everyday life are occasions for growing closer to God, for serving others, and for improving society.

Jacques and Raïssa Maritain. The stories of the Maritains especially struck me, since I was fascinated with nineteenth-century French literature and culture—but this time the scene described was of Parisian salons filled with philosophers discussing Catholic theology!

Subsequent meetings unfolded for me the greatest of treasures: the Eucharist. For twenty-three years, I did not know that the Eucharist, the Communion I received, was the actual Body and Blood of Christ. I heard presenter Tim Staples (another convert) talk about the Eucharistic miracles that could convert the staunchest of skeptics. He pleaded with us: "Cradle Catholics, you have to share these miracles with others!" In the miracle of Lanciano, Italy, God in His great compassion allowed a Host to turn into cardiac tissue and blood to help the unbelief of a priest. This tissue and blood are still fresh thirteen centuries later! God's love for us is so great that He would humble himself to take on the appearance of bread to be closer to us. As I began to study the life of Saint Teresa of Avila, I felt that God was calling me to follow Him as radically as I had once dreamed as a child. I wanted to give Him my love in return for the love He had for me.

My sister, Diana, who was also at UCLA, had also succumbed to humanist and Marxist teachings, being openly critical of the Catholic faith. I shared with her a book that a friend from Opus Dei recommended: *Theology for Beginners* by Frank Sheed.[2] The book was an instrument to begin to bring my sister back to the Church. Our newfound zeal for the Catholic faith brought us closer and made us practically inseparable. One morning while having coffee in our neighborhood coffee shop, we noticed a group of protestors across the street. They were pro-lifers praying outside the local abortion clinic. We decided to go over and talk with them. Five minutes later,

[2] *Theology for Beginners* (New York: Sheed and Ward, 1957).

we were both holding pro-life signs! That was our first encounter with the pro-life movement. I did not know that in America, we were killing close to four thousand unborn children daily. The cause of the unborn grew in my heart, and they were often the first thing on my mind when I woke up in the morning. My sister and I became actively involved in the pro-life movement as sidewalk counselors, pregnancy center volunteers, speakers—and sometimes even pro-life street preachers!

In 2000, when I was at the church where I attended daily Mass, I found a flyer announcing the opening of a pro-life pregnancy center in the Pico-Union district of Los Angeles, the same neighborhood where Diana and I grew up. We both became involved with Los Angeles Pregnancy Services (LAPS) as volunteer counselors (my sister would later become their executive director in 2003, as would I in 2006). I was astonished to discover that this was in fact Los Angeles' abortion ground zero. Seven abortion centers were killing children in close proximity to the very streets of my childhood memories. I could have easily been one of these casualties. My parents could have been one of so many desperate couples who enter the abortion clinics every day. God's providence had taken my life full circle.

On March 2, 2009, at the chapel of EWTN in Alabama and with ten other pro-life activists, I made my promises as a Missionary of the Gospel of Life, a lay association founded by Father Frank Pavone of Priests for Life. It was one of the happiest and most meaningful moments of my life. God never gave up on me and never forgot me. His loving hand protected me and gently guided me from the moment I was conceived. I will never stop fighting for the unborn, and I hope to see an end to the tragedy of abortion in my lifetime.

My Search within the Church

Mary Dudley, West Bloomfield, Michigan

Stories of conversion and reversion to the Catholic faith have always intrigued me. My home library contains many books on the topic. I am fascinated by the various ways people have come to know Christ and by the courage it takes to describe the process. Exposing past mistakes and sins requires a level of bravery that does not come easily. But when it can serve to inspire others to a new and deeper relationship with God, it is a challenge worth taking on. When Teresa asked me to consider contributing to her book about spiritual makeovers, I had already begun praying for the grace to discern whether this was the time to share my own journey of renewal in the faith. Her invitation seemed like a positive answer.

I am a cradle Catholic who never left the Church. Raised in a strong Catholic home, I felt comfortable with the faith my parents modeled. Their example of active participation in both parish and civic matters became the standard I hoped to meet and surpass. I became active in the pro-life movement in the late 1960s, several years before the *Roe v. Wade* decision made abortion on demand the law of the land in our country. The pro-life movement began in hopes of fending off such laws. Although I frequently failed throughout high school and college in my resolve to sin no more and avoid the near occasion of sin, I was confident that the fullness of truth was in the Catholic Church. Attacks against her teachings annoyed me and inspired me to defend their validity. But adequate preparation is critical for that task, and my formation of conscience and knowledge of the faith were dangerously incomplete—although I thought otherwise at the time. The seemingly clear moral teachings I heard about at home seemed to be challenged everywhere I looked. The issue of contraception was particularly confusing. Even though I could recite the rules, I knew no clear reasons why contraception was always wrong and unhealthy for all marriages, regardless of the spouses' religious affiliations. My familiarity with *Humanae Vitae* was limited to the occasional mocking references to the encyclical that I heard at school and on television and the angry reactions from my parents the comments provoked. My parents' responses did not include enough explanations to satisfy my questions, and, sadly, it never occurred to me actually to read the document. In college I came to know many enthusiastic non-Catholic pro-lifers who shared my love for Jesus and my passionate opposition to abortion. They seemed enviably unburdened by the Catholic prohibition of contraception and had no problem with the concept of limiting family size using artificial birth control. The few articles I came across in pro-life literature suggesting a link between abortion and contraception were unconvincing. Perhaps I simply did not want to be convinced. Gradually I came to the conclusion that the Church's teaching against artificial birth control was meant to be self-disciplinary and only for Catholics. Prior to my marriage engagement, I decided that I would follow the rules myself and steer clear of discussing contraception when battling the abortion issue.

Although I went to daily Mass and considered myself a strong Catholic, the confusing messages in the world combined with inadequate conscience formation began to impact my thinking. I was slowly becoming one of those pro-life

Catholics who bought into the faith except for that one "minor" issue of contraception.

My resolve to follow the rules began to weaken after the premarriage counseling session I attended with my fiancé. The priest patiently listened to our concerns about my young age and my desire to finish college and attend law school. I also mentioned my potential for reproductive problems because of exposure to a prescribed medication my mother took while pregnant with me. He was impressed that I had already begun to learn and follow the Natural Family Planning techniques for recognizing signs of fertility in my monthly cycle, and he smiled as we inquired whether this would be our only option to delay and limit family size.

The priest gently told us that we were admirable in our desire to please God and would be greatly blessed. He affirmed that our concerns were legitimate. He proceeded to "correct" our misunderstanding of Church teaching, assuring us that as long as we continued to submit the matter to prayer we could confidently follow the conclusions of our consciences, even if they seemed to conflict with doctrine. After all, he told us, the Church has always taught that personal conscience reigns supreme. He indicated no need for ongoing conscience formation and suggested no tools for it other than prayer, weekly Mass, and occasional reconciliation. The priest left us convinced that Natural Family Planning was just one of many options to consider in our future married life.

We began our marriage under that taint of ignorance and sin. I continued to monitor my fertility but also incorporated noninvasive, nonchemical means to delay pregnancy. Interiorly I often battled feelings of disgust and guilt. But I was also intrigued on a scientific level. I studied to learn more about the effectiveness and dangers of all contraceptive measures. I eventually began incorporating facts about the abortifacient nature of some birth control methods into my pro-life discussions. My spiritual immaturity, however, took an emotional toll. I began an unhealthy pattern of praying that God would understand our decision to avoid pregnancy, followed by increasing spiritual discomfort, shame, and fear, topped off with trips to the confessional where priests would reassure me of my choice. With the grace of the Sacrament, I would try anew to follow only natural means. After failing in these efforts, I would attempt to avoid the topic altogether. I privately cried many tears. Rather than recognize that my conscience, albeit poorly formed, was properly correcting me, I chose to immerse myself more actively in antiabortion activity and volunteer regularly for parish events.

Ironically, when we eventually decided to start a family, I experienced the difficulties conceiving and carrying babies to term. We lost three babies to miscarriage, but we were miraculously blessed with three healthy children, the last of whom was born four months prematurely. That pregnancy had been in crisis from the onset and kept me confined to bed rest for most of its twenty-three weeks. After my preemie was born, as he struggled to survive in the hospital, I struggled to understand God's plan, even to the point of immaturely questioning how He could have let this crisis happen to me after all I had been doing to save unborn babies. The answer He provided by way of a phone call became a precursor to the spiritual overhaul God was preparing for me. A middle-aged, longtime pro-lifer called to let me know of her prayers for my baby, but she unsettled me with the statement "It is so beautiful and fitting that God would choose you to experience this great gift." This was the first time I had considered that our crisis was a gift from God and that He had chosen *me* to receive it. As I prayed about that perspective, my uncertainty and fear began to give way to an increasing trust that my baby was in God's hands. Unfortunately, it did not carry over into my fears about future pregnancies.

As the 1980s came to a close, my husband and I moved our family to Orlando, Florida, where he could launch a new golf-related business. We chose to live in an area close to the famous resorts. That decision landed us in one of the most Eucharistic and Marian parish communities I have ever encountered. The holiness of the priests and parishioners at Holy Family was immediately noticeable. I often told family and friends in Michigan that we could not have found a better place to raise our children in the faith. It was through my participation in that parish that my spiritual makeover took place. Brochures in the back of church about Natural Family Planning caught my attention, as did the Irish priests who gently preached about fidelity to the Church in all matters. I attended question-and-answer sessions where others sought clarification regarding tough moral issues; I was fearful that I would hear that my conscience had led me astray after all. I had long since stopped bringing up birth control in Confession since no priest seemed compelled to correct what I thought were prayerful choices. But my discomfort continued and began to grow. I went to daily Mass begging God for clarity and courage. His answer came in a series of events that changed my marriage, my prayer life, and my relationship with our Lord.

I felt a sudden need to alter our family prayer routine as Lent approached. Even though our children were still quite young, I suggested to my husband that we incorporate more-structured prayers as we prepared them for bed each night. Prior to our move to Florida, I had heard about the Divine Mercy messages Jesus had revealed to Saint Faustina in the 1930s. My parents and brother had been strongly encouraging me to pray the accompanying Chaplet of Divine Mercy during our nightly routine. The children's enthusiastic reaction came with interesting questions that led me to read *Divine Mercy in My Soul*, wherein Saint Faustina records Jesus' revelations about His mercy and love. I began to realize that my fears about pregnancy stemmed from a serious lack of trust in God. And that lack of trust was displeasing to our Lord. But I was still trapped in a fearful mind-set reminiscent of the famous prayer of Saint Augustine, "Give me faith, but not yet."

My growing interest in the Divine Mercy led to conversations at church where I heard about a Catholic nun in Alabama who had started a television network that carried programs about faith matters, including the Divine Mercy. It was called EWTN—Eternal Word Television Network— and I was advised to tune in. I was skeptical and reluctant to do so. As a communications major in college, I had done an internship at a religious television station, and I was familiar with the low-budget, poor-quality productions offered by both Protestant and Catholic groups. But one morning, while the children were in school, I decided on a whim to put on EWTN while I did housework. Since I would be dusting in the back of the house, I turned up the volume. I will never forget the moment I heard blaring from the television that contraception was never permissible and that many couples had been wrongly led astray by trusted priests who were confused by or disagreed with Church teaching. I raced to the TV to see who was speaking and discovered that representatives from the Pontifical Council for the Family were guests of the foundress of EWTN, Mother Angelica, on her talk show. At once I felt a rush of freedom as well as shame because I knew they were right and had to admit to myself that I had known it all along. Why else had I been unable to shake the interior reservations and anxiety I had carried for so long? In tears I resolved to speak to my husband right away, to confess finally with the intent to change, to use only Natural Family Planning and to trust God completely with the gift of my fertility, for which I now had a newfound appreciation.

The Lord was not yet finished with answering my prayers for clarity and the grace to trust Him. I had been making friends with the priests in our parish, hoping to find the courage to seek regular spiritual direction. I had heard about its benefits from fellow classmates in the adult apologetics class I had recently joined. When our pastor announced the reassignment of some of my favorite priests, I thought I had lost my chance to seek spiritual direction. But at a Sunday morning Mass I looked up from my prayers and watched the new associate pastor walk to the altar to assist distributing Holy Communion. I had never seen him before and did not even know his name yet. A sudden rush of God's love came over me and I was aware of an inner voice telling me that here was the priest for whom I had waited. When I later learned that this elderly priest from Ireland, a Jesuit, would be leading interested laypeople in the Spiritual Exercises of Saint Ignatius Loyola, I immediately signed up. The blessings of Father O'Holohan's guidance remain with me to this day, and I am eternally grateful to God. This priest's direction helped me to deepen my love for Jesus and find peace that strengthened the bonds of my marriage. He also helped me find clarity regarding the link between a contraceptive mentality and the culture's unwillingness to protect unborn babies from abortion. It was from Father O'Holohan that I received the audiocassette of Professor Janet Smith's talk "Contraception: Why Not?" He also encouraged me to read papal encyclicals, beginning with John Paul II's *Familiaris Consortio*. I was finally able to see the tragic short-circuiting of the pro-life cause due to the refusal by so many to explore and articulate the beautiful and authoritative teachings so brilliantly expressed in John Paul II's writings as well as in Paul VI's *Humanae Vitae.* I still struggle occasionally to trust God in all matters of my life. In fact, several years ago, when our family jokingly created descriptive Native American names for each other after watching the movie *Dances with Wolves*, I could hardly object to their choice for me: "Worst-Case Scenario". But I know that the spiritual overhaul God initiated in me over twenty years ago continues to bear fruit. He has provided opportunities for me to serve Him as a spiritual mentor, a study group facilitator, a morning host on Catholic radio, and a pro-life public speaker. He has blessed my husband and me with a strong marriage and three grown children who are deeply committed to the Catholic faith, two of whom hold graduate degrees in theology. God is good.

Clay in the Hands of the
Ultimate Makeover Artist

There is no better place for a woman to be than in the arms of Christ within the Catholic Church. The teachings and traditions He gives us through Catholicism are able to turn cracked pots like me, Nina, Kathy, Mary Lockwood, Janet, Astrid, and Mary Dudley into incredible works of art. God is ready and waiting to perform that same extreme makeover miracle in your life, or the life of someone you know.

It could be that you have a strong relationship with God and love the Church. Keep growing. Keep learning and keep educating yourself about the faith, as well as about cultural influences that continue to attack our core beliefs. Do what you can to help those around you who are struggling in their walk.

Maybe you have a friend, a sister, or a daughter who has fallen away from the Church. Maybe you are slowly trying to make your way back into a relationship with God. Maybe you've been in a tug-of-war with Jesus over particular issues and are afraid to let go. Have faith. Pray and do not lose heart. You've read my story and the stories of others who have gone into the spiritual spa kicking and screaming but came out brand-new, shining creatures for Christ. Again, nothing is impossible with God. He loves us and wants you to be the best you can be. We can allow ourselves to be clay in the Potter's hands, or we can walk away.

The choice is yours. I hope and pray that you choose— and keep choosing—Christ.

The word that came to Jeremiah from the LORD: "Arise, and go down to the potter's house, and there I will let you hear my words." So I went down to the potter's house, and there he was working at his wheel. And the vessel he was making of clay was spoiled in the potter's hand, and he reworked it into another vessel, as it seemed good to the potter to do.

Then the word of the LORD came to me: "O house of Israel, can I not do with you as this potter has done? says the LORD. Behold, like the clay in the potter's hand, so are you in my hand, O house of Israel."

—Jeremiah 18:1–6